MOVING TO PALM BEACH COUNTY

THE UN-TOURIST GUIDE®

D1256775

MARIAN WHITE

To Justin—out of the 1.3 million people in Palm Beach County, you're my favorite.

"It is my plan to create a city that is direct and simple... To leave out all that is ugly, to eliminate the unnecessary, and to give Florida and the nation a resort city as perfect as study and ideals can make it."

Addison Mizner
Palm Beach County's legendary architect in 1925

CONTENTS

WELCOME HOME

When longtime locals hear the words "Palm Beach," they think of home—a place to live comfortably, sun frequently, and dine exceptionally—and they're not alone.

Source: Discover the Palm Beaches
Palm Beach

As a recent Palm Beach County transplant, I can attest that Palm Beach is coastal living at its finest. It's morning walks on the beach and afternoon drinks on the patio. It's a thriving job market and an array of quality schools. It's gilded seaside mansions and shabby beach bungalows. It's farmers market Saturdays and sandbar Sundays. And most importantly, it's home to 1.3 million people of every age, religion, and background you can think of—all of whom have their own version of life in Palm Beach.

Yet, for potential newcomers, the tony town known as Palm Beach may paint a limited image—one etched with dapper men in smoking slippers and posh women in sun hats—all of whom are most certainly sipping Veuve Clicquot at this very moment. After all, Palm Beach socialite and heiress, Marjorie Merriweather Post, stated that there was *"more money, more champagne, more caviar, more Rolls-Royces, and of course, more affluence in Palm Beach than in all the rest of America put together."*

I myself must admit that I was guilty of having this singular view of "Palm Beach" before moving here in 2015. That winter, my husband's Boston-headquartered firm gave us the opportunity to relocate to its growing West Palm Beach office. All it took was a glance outside at our snow-globe surroundings for us to quickly trade our over-priced, one-bedroom apartment in chilly Boston for a spacious, three-story townhome by the beach in sunny Palm Beach County.

Source: Discover the Palm Beaches
Aerial view of West Palm Beach and Palm Beach

So, after months of house hunting and planning, I quit my steady journalism job, hopped on a plane, and moved to Palm Beach. It's one of the best decisions I've ever made—and I am confident that you will feel the same soon enough.

While the fabled town of Palm Beach certainly lives up to its illustrious depiction, I quickly discovered that the famous barrier island only scratches the surface of all of the amazing things that this county has to offer. What I now call "home"—the Palm Beaches—is rich in history and culture. Its 38 different municipalities are filled with both celebrities and everyday families, yachts and fishing boats, bankers and farmers, urban downtowns and suburban metropolises, yuppies and retirees, bargain antiques and high-end shopping, tennis courts and wetlands. And yes—it's true—some very crazy drivers.

Source: Lila Photo
Sunday brunch at the International Polo Club

Since moving here, I've also learned just as much about what to do as I have about what *not* to do when it comes to relocating to the Palm Beach area. My goal is to help make your move as smooth as possible, so that you can skip the relocation headaches and jump head-first into Palm Beach County's fantastic communities. Many of them, as you'll learn, are even the proud recipients of media recognitions and laudations, including "Most Fun Small Town in America," "Top 100 Places to Live," and "America's Happiest Seaside Town."

So kick off the Uggs and slip on those sandals. It's time to start living the good life, here in Palm Beach County.

Top 10 Reasons Why You Will Love Calling Palm Beach County Home

#1 You Can Kiss Winter Goodbye

In Palm Beach, the locals will tell you they'd rather *"salt their margaritas than salt their driveways."* You can say goodbye to thermals and long underwear (the stuff nightmares are made of) and say hello to tank tops, shorts, and flip-flops. While you may occasionally need a sweater or light jacket, you'll very rarely need a heavy coat in Palm Beach County's balmy 74 degree winters. All of this means you'll spend less time layering up and more time outdoors enjoying all that the area has to offer.

#2 There Is So Much To Do Outdoors

Forget hibernating during the winter months—here in Palm Beach you can spend much or part of every day outside. From tennis and golf to water sports and long walks on the beach, you have endless outdoor recreational options. With nearly 50 miles of stunning coastline and brilliant blue ocean warmed by the Gulf Stream, the area is also a boating, diving, and snorkeling paradise. Did I mention there are 81 parks filled with bike paths, walking paths, and campsites?

Source: Discover the Palm Beaches
Residents bike Palm Beach's popular Lake Trail

12

#3 Golf Capital of the World

If you don't play golf yet, you will in Palm Beach. We are well-known as the preeminent golf capital of the world and home to the Professional Golfers Association of America (PGA). With warm weather year-round, everyday golfers and professional golfers alike have approximately 160 public and private golf course options to choose from on a daily basis. Golf enthusiasts can also witness world famous golf tournaments in their own backyards. Many of golf's biggest celebrities have made Palm Beach County their home, including Michelle Wie, Jack Nicklaus, and Tiger Woods.

#4 Shop 'Til You Drop

With countless shopping centers, department stores, and high-end boutiques, it's easy to see why Palm Beach County is truly a shopping mecca for everyone. Take a window-shopping stroll by Worth Avenue's high-end stores or hunt down beautiful antiques in West Palm's charming Antique Row District. Don't forget Boca Raton's Town Center or The Gardens Mall in Palm Beach Gardens, which are both chock-full of every kind of retail store imaginable.

#5 A Thriving Arts Scene

After a short while living here, you'll quickly realize the huge role that art plays in Palm Beach's culture. Area residents have a genuine appreciation for and love of the arts. With more than 17 performing art centers, Palm Beach regularly hosts world-famous artists, musicians, and performers. Downtown West Palm Beach's Kravis Center for the Performing Arts boasts everything from international symphony orchestras and the Miami City Ballet to Broadway hits and stand-up comedy. In addition to the performing arts, the Norton Museum of Art also features both Contemporary and European Art. To catch a glimpse into Palm Beach's thriving arts scene, locals can also explore Delray's Arts Garage and West Palm's historic Northwood Village – both of which only help to further stimulate Palm Beach County's stellar economy.

#6 Life Is One Big Festival

Get your party hat ready because life really is one big festival here in Palm Beach. Thousands flock to the area every year for dozens of exciting fairs and festivals throughout the county. In addition to anchor events like the South Florida Fair, the Palm Beach International Boat Show, and SunFest, Palm Beach County also hosts numerous art, music, and food festivals throughout the year. From the Palm Beach Food & Wine Fest and the Delray Bacon & Bourbon Fest to the Festival of the Arts BOCA and the Palm Beach Holiday Boat Parade, you can always find a celebration happening here.

Source: Festival Management Group and VMA Studios
Delray Affair is the largest arts & crafts festival in the Southeast U.S.

#7 Living Here Doesn't Have to Break the Bank

Despite the fact that Palm Beach County happens to be the wealthiest county in Florida, it is actually affordable and accessible to just about anyone, including those of us without deep pockets and fat bank accounts. While not everyone can afford a million-dollar Ocean Boulevard home, many of us can afford to rent or buy a home in places like Jupiter, Palm Beach Gardens, West Palm Beach, Lake Worth, Delray Beach, Boynton Beach or Boca Raton. With countless housing options and a cost of living well below that of other major East Coast cities like DC, Boston, and NYC, you can live within your means in Palm Beach.

#8 Fantastic Schools

Whether it's a nationally recognized public school or an award-winning private academy, you will find the right school for you and your kids here in Palm Beach County. Our schools and universities are unmatched. Palm Beach County's much-lauded school district boasts one of the country's most extensive advanced studies options including: Advanced Placement (AP); International Baccalaureate (IB); middle school Pre-IB; Science, Technology, Engineering, and Math (STEM); and Cambridge University's Advanced International Certificate of Education (AICE), according to the Business Development Board of Palm Beach County.

Source: Dana McMahon
Shopping along Worth Avenue in Palm Beach

Source: Carl Dawson of LivingExposure and the
Delray Beach Downtown Development Authority
Evening on "the Ave." in Delray Beach

#9 A Stellar Economy

Palm Beach enjoys a thriving economy, thanks in large part to the area's phenomenal technology, business, and tourism industries, which generate thousands of jobs throughout the county. In addition to a strong job market, the area's stellar economy has also led to increased development and improvements in Palm Beach County's various towns. Revitalized cities like Delray Beach and West Palm Beach have both undergone dramatic facelifts in the last decade. Thankfully, it looks as though this positive economic trend will only continue, which means Palm Beach County towns will keep getting better and better.

#10 Pet Friendly Environment

Palm Beach County is truly a pet owner's paradise. Not only do we have an ideal climate and plenty of parks for outdoor pets, but many of our county's pet-tolerant rental policies also make it especially easy for Palm Beachers to own a cat or dog. In fact, the majority of apartment and condo rentals in the area—from Jupiter down to Boca Raton—are described as "pet-friendly." Furthermore, the Palm Beach County area also boasts a number of pet-friendly hotels, dog parks, and restaurants, where folks can dine al-fresco, leash in-hand.

CHAPTER 1

A BRIEF HISTORY OF PALM BEACH COUNTY

"This place was nothing but a wilderness when we came here in 1876, but how beautiful that wilderness was."

– Ella Geer Dimick, Lake Worth pioneer

Today, the island of "Palm Beach" embodies a tropical, palm tree-lined paradise. However, less than 200 years ago, this ideal isle was nothing more than a small territory of sand and vegetation. The surrounding areas – what would become Palm Beach County in full—were swampy and buggy terrain, inhabited mainly by mosquitos, snakes, and alligators. It's safe to say that Palm Beach was far from paradise.

Early Beginnings

Our county's early Native Americans first came into contact with western settlers in 1513, when Spanish explorer and conquistador Juan Ponce de Leon made his historic landfall in "La Florida." By 1763, however, the British had gained control of the entire Florida territory.

From 1818 to 1858, the bloody "Seminole Wars" played out between the Seminole Indians and settlers throughout Florida, with the Battles of Loxahatchee taking place in Palm Beach County's northern regions. After the Third Seminole War ended, the remaining Native Americans fled deep into the Everglades to avoid being forced West into the official Indian Territory. For years, Native Americans hid out in South Florida's nearby swamps.

FUN FACT

By the 1950s the Seminole and Miccosukee Indians created the Seminole Tribe of Florida and were recognized by the U.S. as a sovereign nation in 1961.

Pioneers Pave the Way for Palm Beach County

In 1872, the first pioneers arrived in Palm Beach County, settling near—what is known today as—the Lake Worth Lagoon. At the time, the entire Palm Beach area was known as "Lake Worth Country," named after Colonel William Jenkins Worth, who brought the Second Seminole War to a close in 1842. Pioneer life was, to say the least, taxing. Living amongst wild animals, dense jungle-like surroundings, and an overall treacherous environment, these pioneers somehow fought the odds to settle successfully in the future Palm Beaches.

Palm Beach in 1929

FUN FACT

It is also the pioneers who are to thank for coining our beloved island's name. In 1878, the "Providencia," a ship bound from Cuba to Barcelona, washed ashore on the Palm Beaches, and with it, a flood of coconuts. Thanks to the planting of these coconuts, palm trees popped up everywhere on the island—hence our region's namesake.

Near the end of the 19th Century, word spread that Lake Worth was a paradise of sorts. Not only was the area a warmer alternative to the frigid winters up north, but the county was also becoming a real community with a hotel called the "Cocoanut House," a church, and a post office. By the late 1800s, more than 200 people called Lake Worth home.

FUN FACT

The iconic Jupiter Inlet Lighthouse stands as the oldest building in Palm Beach County. Construction on the lighthouse began in the 1850s but wasn't completed until 1860.

Henry Flagler and the Florida East Coast Railroad

In 1894, the "Pioneer Era" officially ended with the opening of Henry Morrison Flagler's Royal Poinciana Hotel in Palm Beach and the debut of the Florida East Coast Railroad. Flagler, who was a partner in Standard Oil with John D. Rockefeller, would come to be known as the "father of Palm Beach." The visionary implemented a grand plan to transform the island into a resort playground for the wealthy, along with a separate town to the west of the lake—now known as West Palm Beach—for the working class laborers, who would be working in these Palm Beach hotels.

The Breakers today in Palm Beach

FUN FACT

The inspiration for and precursor to today's SunFest in West Palm Beach began in 1916 with a three-day annual event called the Seminole Sun Dance. The festival took place with Indian street dances and music on Clematis Street.

During the glamorous Gilded Age, Henry Flagler also built The Palm Beach Inn, now known as The Breakers. This iconic Palm Beach hotel burned to the ground—not once, but twice—over the course of several decades. It was later rebuilt as an even more magnificent structure and renamed "The Breakers" due to tourists' commonly referring to it as the hotel "down by the breakers."

In addition to transporting wealthy visitors to the island of Palm Beach, the Florida East Coast Railroad also made it possible to transport necessary commodities to the locals at a much quicker pace. Likewise, it allowed the Palm Beach region to ship its own agricultural products to northern states more efficiently. With tracks connecting multiple towns along the coast, Flagler's railroad truly ushered in a new era for Palm Beach County. Several nearby towns grew and developed as a direct result of the Florida East Coast Railroad's influence on the area.

One such town was Boynton Beach, whose residents were suddenly able to ship their locally-grown fruits and vegetables up to the northern cities. Today, the railroad is still a daily part of the Palm Beach County way of life. Locals see and hear the trains numerous times a week as they rush across several bustling areas of the county, including Delray Beach's popular Atlantic Avenue.

Source: The Boca Raton Historical Society
Frank Chesebro's pineapple plantation in Boca Raton, 1903

FUN FACT

Originally, Delray Beach was called "Linton," after the U.S. Congressman William Linton, who bought land in the community. After 1898, many settlers left the area including William Linton, himself. The town's name was changed to "Delray" in 1901, translating to "of the king" in Spanish.

The Palm Beach County Land Boom

The separate, proletariat town of West Palm Beach was laid out by George Potter, who planned a 48-block area spanning from Lake Worth to Clear Lake. Other notable Palm Beach names from this time include: Franklin Sheen, engineer for Model Land Company and for West Palm Beach; James Marion Owens, who was responsible for building both Flagler's grand estate, Whitehall, and parts of the

Royal Poinciana Hotel; E.R. Bradley, who from 1898 to 1945, owned the Beach Club, an illegal gambling casino in Palm Beach.

FUN FACT

Henry Flagler had his famous Whitehall mansion built for his third wife, Mary Lily Kenan. The mansion is now listed on the National Register of Historic Places and is open to the public as the Flagler Museum.

In 1894, West Palm Beach became the first incorporated town in South Florida. It wasn't until 1911 that its well-heeled sister town of Palm Beach was officially incorporated into Palm Beach County.

After Flagler's death in 1913, growth and development escalated in West Palm Beach, resulting in a significant building boom in the county. Schools, businesses, and churches popped up constantly as more and more newcomers flocked to the county. The growing need for these buildings resulted in a steep increase in construction and infrastructure, often referred to as the famous 1920's Land Boom.

Architect Addison Mizner's Impact on Palm Beach County

American architect and Palm Beach legend Addison Mizner moved to our county in 1918, forever changing the region's look and feel. Upon arriving in Palm Beach, Mizner found that the predominant architectural style on the island reflected the flashy Gilded-Age. The architect imagined a more subtropical-appropriate look for the area's buildings, with new Mediterranean and Spanish style architecture.

Today, this timeless style has been dubbed "the Palm Beach Look," and can be seen in the various stucco homes and Spanish tile roofs throughout South Florida.

Mizner's first major Palm Beach development was the Spanish-mission-style Everglades Club, which remains one of the most exclusive country clubs in Palm Beach today. Mizner also designed several Palm Beach mansions for various oligarchs, including El Mirasol (demolished in the 1950s), La Bellucia (sold for $24 million in 2009), Villa Flora, and La Guerida (became the "Winter White House" for President Kennedy, often called the Kennedy Compound). As more private homes and mansions were built, the mega-wealthy began looking to make Palm Beach their winter home

FUN FACT

Only two marked graves exist in Palm Beach today, and they both belong to Addison Mizner's pets. The more famous of which was his spider monkey, Johnnie Brown. The monkey's grave is located in Via Mizner on Worth Avenue.

In 1925, Mizner set out to build the spectacular Ritz-Carlton Cloister Inn, now known as the world-famous Boca Raton Resort & Club. Mizner hoped to transform Boca Raton into a true resort destination, with the creation of his oceanfront hotel, golf courses, and residential community. Today, Addison Mizner's name can be seen throughout the Palm Beaches on schools, buildings, and parks. Boca Raton even has a Mizner Park, a Mizner Boulevard, and an Addison Mizner Elementary School—all to commemorate South Florida's most memorable architect.

Source: The Boca Raton Historical Society
A vintage 1930s postcard of the Boca Raton Resort & Club

Of course, by the end of the 1920's Land Boom, this dramatic growth and development stopped dead in its tracks due to a myriad of problems. In addition to the Great Depression and other economic factors, a deadly force of nature also was to blame for Palm Beach County's decline: the infamous Okeechobee Hurricane. In September 1928, the category 4 hurricane swept through the region, killing around 3,000 people and causing massive flood and wind damage.

The Resurgence of Palm Beach County

After facing a steep decline, Palm Beach County managed to reemerge as a burgeoning and prosperous metropolitan area. The '50s, '60s, and '70s witnessed an influx of retirees moving to Florida and snatching up second homes in the area. During the 1950s, West Palm Beach quickly became one of the fastest growing areas of the country.

This growth continued but was stalled by West Palm Beach's high crime rates in the 1970s and 1980s. Many people chose to move outside of West Palm Beach, opting for nearby suburban towns, leaving West Palm's downtown dilapidated and vacant for the most part.

FUN FACT

In the 1970's, George Morikami donated his land to the county in honor of the Japanese Yamato Colony. Today, the colony is commemorated in the Morikami Museum and Japanese Gardens in Delray Beach, as well as Yamato Road in Boca Raton.

Things began to turn around for West Palm Beach in the 1990s, however, with major developments like CityPlace's shops and restaurants and Clematis Street's many renovations. These improvements led to a revival of the city's downtown scene, attracting a wave of young professionals to West Palm Beach's new apartment and condo developments.

Historic neighborhoods in West Palm, such as El Cid and Flamingo Park, have also experienced a revitalization in the past few decades. Surrounding towns like Delray Beach, Lake Worth, and Boynton

Beach have experienced—and are still undergoing—a major resurgence, with new shopping districts, parks, and restaurants now lining the cities once-neglected streets.

FUN FACT

Much of Bernie Madoff's infamous ponzi scheme dealings took place at the local Palm Beach Country Club, where he preyed on quite a few of the county's richest residents.

Of course, the 2008 economic recession did stall, and even halt, various developments and projects throughout the area. The economic slowdown also negatively affected many of the county's neighborhood property values. Lately though, many of these stalled residential and commercial projects have picked back up where they left off. Condo buildings, restaurants, and storefronts continue to pop up seemingly daily in places like Delray Beach, Jupiter, and West Palm Beach.

This quick synopsis only offers a glimpse into Palm Beach County's fascinating and complex history. With area towns getting better and better and a growing population that continues to diversify, this region of the country will continue to make history.

For more background on the region, I recommend checking out the Johnson History Museum and Historical Society of Palm Beach County, located in West Palm Beach. www.historicalsocietypbc.org

CHAPTER 2
NAVIGATING PALM BEACH COUNTY

"While there are few bad views from State Road A1A anywhere along the coast, once north of the pomp of Palm Beach, the back-to-nature scenery is downright stunning, and reminders of Florida's much-ignored history abound."

— New Times Broward-Palm Beach

Out of the 20 million people who live in the State of Florida, 1.3 million of them are lucky enough to call Palm Beach County home. The county's sprawling 2,000-plus square miles of land encompasses a vast array of wildlife, interweaving waterways, and nearly 50 miles of glistening Atlantic coastline. Not only is the area the third most populous county in Florida (behind Miami-Dade and Broward Counties), but it is also one of the largest counties, size-wise, in the eastern United States. In fact, Palm Beach County is larger than both Rhode Island and Delaware.

Palm Beach County Nicknames

You'll commonly hear locals refer to this shoreline as the "Gold Coast," which stretches from Palm Beach all the way down to our rowdier southern neighbors, Fort Lauderdale and Miami. Some believe the nickname "Gold Coast" refers to the area's long history of shipwrecks and supposed sunken loot, while others will tell you it alludes to the population's ritzy lifestyle and wealthy residents. You will also hear locals refer to the area as "The Treasure Coast," which typically encompasses Palm Beach and its northern neighbors—Martin, St. Lucie, and Indian River counties. Most often, however, you'll hear the county referred to as simply, "The Palm Beaches."

A Geographic Guide

Locals break this very large county into four distinct regions: North County, Central County, South County, and "the Glades" (or West County). Along the county's coastline you'll find the Atlantic Coastal Ridge, which appears as a string of barrier islands. These barrier islands are home to many of Palm Beach County's wealthiest communities including, of course, Palm Beach, as well as Manalapan, Ocean Ridge, Gulf Stream, and the eastern parts of Delray Beach and Boca Raton.

As for our neighbors, Palm Beach County borders Broward County to the south, Hendry County to the west, and Martin County to the north. In the northwest corner, Palm Beach County also borders and shares Lake Okeechobee with Glades and Okeechobee Counties.

Source: Discover the Palm Beaches
Royal Poinciana Way in Palm Beach

A little rundown on Lake Okeechobee

- Palm Beach locals commonly refer to it as "Florida's Inland Sea" and "The Lake."

- Its name is actually taken from the Seminole Indian language, appropriately translating to "big water."

- Lake Okeechobee is 730 square miles of surface area, and it's also the largest lake in the southeastern United States.

- Lake Okeechobee is a key resource for South Florida's freshwater supply and flood control systems.

Source: www.sfwmd.gov

Getting Around by Car

Navigating a new place, let alone one of the largest counties in the U.S., can be intimidating. But rest assured—if I can do it, so can you. Here's what you need to know before zipping through the county.

Source: Dana McMahon
Traffic crosses the Royal Park Bridge in Palm Beach and West Palm Beach

Roads to Know

Unlike Manhattan or Boston, where one can easily live without a vehicle, it is fairly important to have a car when living and working in the Palm Beaches. There's no subway, and the county's towns are quite spread out. Chances are good that you may choose to live in a town where you aren't working, so it's best to have a safe and reliable car to get you there.

The Florida Turnpike and Interstate 95 both run the length of the county and are essential for commuters. U.S. Highway One (Route One), Dixie Highway, Military Trail, State Roads 441, Southern Boulevard, and Coastal Highway A1A are all important thoroughfares to know.

Expect more traffic and congested roads during the high season, which usually starts around the holidays and ends by April. Unless you have to commute to work, I recommend avoiding these main thoroughfares during the early morning and early evening hours

Tip for Commuters: If commuting to and from work on Interstate 95, take advantage of the HOV lane during rush hour, between 7 to 9 a.m. and 4 to 6 p.m. on weekdays. To ride in the HOV lane, drivers must have at least two people in the car. *However, there is one exception.* Florida also allows owners of specific hybrid and other low-emission vehicles to ride in the HOV lane by themselves during rush hours. In order to obtain this privilege, owners must register with the state to receive a special decal. Not all hybrid cars receive this special treatment, however. Make sure to check with the **Florida Department of Highway Safety and Motor Vehicles** at www.flhsmv. gov for more information.

Similar to Manhattan, many streets in West Palm Beach's historic areas and in other parts of the county are laid out like a grid. And with names like Clematis, Sapodilla, Evernia, and Datura, you should start noticing a pattern—many of them are also named after plants.

For the most part, "avenues" in the county run north to south, while most "streets" run east to west. This is the case for Boca Raton, Delray Beach, and West Palm Beach – but not the case for Lake Worth or Boynton Beach, where the opposite is true.

In Delray Beach, Atlantic Avenue divides the town into north and south—while Swinton Avenue is the dividing line for east and west. However, in Boca Raton, Dixie Highway is considered the east-west divider.

Getting Around Town

Source: Discover the Palm Beaches
Residents riding the trolley in downtown West Palm Beach

For those without a car, there are other modes of transportation available in Palm Beach County. The **Palm Tran** bus system runs seven days a week throughout the Palm Beaches. All Palm Tran buses contain wheelchair ramps, surveillance cameras, and bike racks. Riders can plan their trip and discover bus routes using the myStop mobile app for iPhone users as well as the website www.palmtran.org/igo, which is also available for Android mobile devices. Reduced fares are available for students, disabled, and senior citizens.

In the city of West Palm Beach, you can get around town using one of the hop-on-hop-off Downtown Trolleys. These trolleys are free and a great way to explore all that West Palm Beach has to offer. West Palm Beach also offers a convenient and popular bike sharing program called **SkyBike WPB**. Customers can rent daily, weekly, monthly, and even, yearly.

For long distance commuters, the **Tri-Rail** train, which connects West Palm Beach to Fort Lauderdale and Miami, is another transportation alternative. For those heading to the airport, Tri-Rail also offers free shuttle bus services between Palm Beach International Airport and Tri-Rail's West Palm Beach Station.

Source: Dana McMahon
Take advantage of our popular bike sharing program, SkyBike

Palm Beach County residents will soon be able to take the **All Aboard Florida**'s upcoming Brightline trains. The service will transport passengers at a speed of up to 125 miles per hour from Miami to Orlando, with a stop in West Palm Beach. All Aboard Florida is expected to open in 2017, with service between Miami and West Palm Beach. Full-service from Miami to Orlando is expected to begin in 2018.

When in downtown Delray Beach or Boca Raton, I highly recommend taking the **Downtowner**. The free, on-demand electric car taxi, which looks like a golf cart and operates similar to Uber, shuttles residents around both of these vibrant downtowns. The service is free but tips are encouraged. The Downtowner mobile app is available for both iPhone and Android. Locals can also hop aboard the **Downtown Roundabout**, which provides free trolley service throughout downtown Delray Beach.

Of course, there are also numerous taxi companies in the area as well as the popular on-demand ride service, Uber.

Getting Out of Town

Palm Beach International Airport (PBI) is by far the best choice when it comes to airport travel in the area. The convenient and manageable airport, which serves six million passengers every year, was voted third best airport in the U.S. and sixth best airport in the world, by *Conde Nast Traveler* in 2014. The airport is centrally located in West Palm Beach, a short drive away from anywhere in the county. PBI has nearly 200 flights daily, with 12 airlines providing nonstop service to numerous destinations, including: Boston, DC, New York, Chicago, and many more. Fort Lauderdale-Hollywood Airport and Miami International Airport provide other nearby flight options as well.

CHAPTER THREE
PALM BEACH SEASONS

"Come high season in January, Palm Beach becomes a playground for the wealthy, who, for a few brief months, stage extravagant charity galas, host six-figure campaign dinners and enjoy wintertime golf, boating and fishing."

– Florida Travel + Life Magazine

From the mix of people to the numerous events and festivals, every aspect of Palm Beach life changes with the seasons, making this an especially interesting place to call home.

**Source: Carl Dawson of LivingExposure and the
Delray Beach Downtown Development Authority
Just another sunny day in the Palm Beaches**

33

West Palm Beach and its surrounding towns have an average year-round temperature of 75 degrees. The area is blessed with a subtropical climate, thanks to the Gulf Stream, which keeps the Palm Beaches warmer during the winter months than the rest of the southeastern United States. Summers are hot, humid, and rainy. Between June and September, expect afternoon rain showers and short-lived thunderstorms almost daily.

Winter, on the other hand, is truly the most wonderful time of the year in the Palm Beaches. From December to April, expect mostly warm, sunny weather that dips into the 60's and, occasionally, into the 40's and 50's at night. Palm Beach's mild winters allow residents to prolong their outdoor activities, like tennis, boating, and golf throughout the entire year. However, the season does experience occasional "cold snaps," making sweaters a necessity.

Here's a quick rundown on the two distinct seasons in Palm Beach County.

"Season" or High Season

Source: Lila Photo
Polo season kicks off at the International Polo Club in Wellington

As a local Palm Beach County resident, you'll quickly become familiar with the area's "season." Specific "season" dates vary depending on who you ask, but typically take place from December to April. Snowbirds and visitors will begin to trickle into the Palm Beaches, starting around the holidays and are usually gone by Mother's Day (mid-May) at the latest. Needless to say, "season" happens to be the busiest time for the Palm Beaches, with numerous festivals, fairs, and events happening weekly throughout the county's various cities.

During season, the Palm Beach social scene also comes alive through glamorous galas and charity fundraisers attended by the crème-de-la-crème, who gloss the pages of *The Palm Beach Daily News* (referred to as "**The Shiny Sheet**" by locals). And, if you're looking to catch a glance of a dashing Argentinian polo player (like **Nacho Figueras**), the high season is your chance to do so. The Palm Beach polo season begins in January and runs through April.

While the high season boasts an abundance of things to do, it does have its cons. Restaurant reservations will be harder to come by, public beaches are packed, traffic is gridlocked, and rental car rates are sky high. Despite these negatives though, you'll gladly wait for a restaurant table in the Palm Beaches once you see the blustery cold that chills the rest of the country.

Low Season

The Palm Beaches' low season begins in May and ends sometime in November. The area empties out in the summer becoming a much more low-key place to live—albeit a much hotter place to live as well.

Tourists flock to the Palm Beaches during the shoulder seasons of April-May and September-November. Not only are the local hotel rates less expensive, but the weather is also still relatively comfortable. June through August are generally the Palm Beaches' hottest months, with high humidity and temps hitting the 80's and 90's.

The advantages of living in Palm Beach County during the low season are that you will get to experience the area's world-renowned restaurants, beaches, and hotels without the crowds. Plus, you won't have to battle bumper-to-bumper traffic on your daily commute.

Source: The Brazilian Court Hotel
The Brazilian Court Hotel in Palm Beach is one of many local hotels
that offer special rates to Florida residents during the low season

Hurricane Season

Florida's dreaded hurricane season happens to align with these hotter months. From June through November, the threat of hurricanes and tropical storms is very real. Thankfully, our community hasn't had to weather a major hurricane in ten years. Of course, this doesn't mean we're in the clear forever.

Palm Beach County last encountered a major storm in 2005 with the destructive Hurricane Wilma, which caused around $20 billion in damages to the area. A year prior, Palm Beach County was struck by both Hurricane Frances and Hurricane Jeanne, two major storms that caused widespread power outages, destruction, and multiple deaths.

Bottom line: As a Palm Beach County resident, it's imperative that you plan ahead of the hurricane season to protect yourself and your home from damage. To do so, I strongly recommend reading **Palm Beach County's Hurricane Survival Guide**, which can be downloaded on the Palm Beach County website at www.pbcgov.com/dem/hurricane. The service provides important emergency numbers and a 26-page comprehensive "survival guide," complete with a checklist and step-by-step instructions on protecting everything from your yard and home to your pet and boat. Make sure you are aware of your evacuation zone and nearest shelters, in case of emergency.

Preparing a disaster supplies kit is also a good idea. Before a storm hits, every household should have at least three days worth of bottled water, non-perishable food, a battery-powered weather radio, extra batteries, flashlights, a first aid kit, tools, a can opener, maps, and prescription medicines. Other supply kit recommendations are listed in the Palm Beach County's Hurricane Survival Guide.

CHAPTER FOUR

THERE'S SO MUCH TO DO OUTDOORS

"There are no other Everglades in the world. They are, they have always been, one of the unique regions of the earth…"

—Marjory Stoneman Douglas, environmentalist and writer

Source: Discover the Palm Beaches
Ocean Reef Park

Living in Palm Beach County is all about the great outdoors. From the sea grape lined beaches to the clay covered tennis courts, the adventures are endless. Here's a look at some of the best places to go and things to do while living in this sunny paradise.

Boating

The ability to boat just about anywhere—from the Intracoastal to the open ocean—is one of the major advantages of living in the Palm Beaches. Two of the most popular boat types in the county are center consoles and sport fishing boats. Of course, don't be surprised if you also see a handful of serious mega-yachts lining Palm Beach's marinas.

Source: Discover the Palm Beaches
A sport fishing boat zips through Palm Beach County

Buying a Boat

Boat buyers have the option of buying a new or pre-owned boat. New boats offer all of the bells and whistles you might expect: new technology, cutting-edge innovation, and desirable warranties. However, high costs are a major con. Many boat experts will recommend purchasing a used boat that is relatively new, that still has a warranty, and has had lots of optional equipment added to it already.

I recommend attending a nearby boat show to experience the varying makes and models in-person. Once the buyer decides on the boat they want, they can sign up for a new build right at the boat show. If purchasing a pre-owned boat or yacht, many Palm Beachers will use a yacht broker. There are numerous yacht brokerage firms available in the Palm Beach area, with plenty of Certified Professional Yacht Brokers to help make your boating dreams come true.

Tips on Buying a Boat in the Palm Beaches

by Steve Gallagher

Whether you are a seasoned yachtsman or novice boater, using a Professional Yacht Broker to represent you and guide you is a smart move that will ultimately save you money and make your boating experience more enjoyable. A boat buyer should consider the broker to be their boating concierge. What may work in New England or The Great Lakes, may not be suited for South Florida and the Bahamas. Once you have identified your mission and your price range, it's time for the fun to start.

When buying a pre-owned boat, it is all about condition, equipment, and engine hours—condition being the most important of the three. I would rather buy a boat with 500 hrs that has been maintained and well cared for than a boat that has 100 hrs and has been sitting around with little use and care. The South Florida sun and salt can quickly take an expensive toll on boats so spending a little more and buying one that has been preserved and taken care of, is often a better investment than trying to restore one that can be bought cheap. That said, almost any boat you buy is going to need something, so be sure to budget a reserve to customize the boat the way you want it or make minor repairs.

Once you have identified the boat you want to buy, your broker will do a market analysis for you so you can decide what you want to offer and what the boat is really worth. After negotiating a deal, use a reputable Marine Surveyor to inspect the boat and make sure everything is in good working order.

Living and boating in Palm Beach and The Bahamas is an enviable way of life that most of the world only dreams of and many consider to be only for the rich. The truth is, you don't have to own a multi-million dollar yacht to enjoy the same lifestyle. Many large yacht owners will be the first to tell you that they have more fun in their little boat than they do with the big boat. There are plenty of boats that are very affordable and very capable of getting you to The Bahamas and beyond. If a large yacht is in your budget and on your bucket list, buy it and go cruising. There is no better lifestyle and the people you meet along the way will become some of your closest friends. It doesn't matter what kind of boat you are buying, the most important thing is to make the time to get out and enjoy it. See you out on the water!

Steve Gallagher of United Yacht Sales is a leading yacht broker in Palm Beach County. When not on the water, Steve enjoys traveling over to The Bahamas with his wife and daughter where they enjoy offshore fishing and freediving. You can reach Steve at <u>SteveG@Unitedyacht.</u> <u>com.</u>

The three major boat shows in South Florida during the season include the **Fort Lauderdale International Boat Show** in November, the **Yachts Miami Beach Show** in February, and the **Palm Beach International Boat Show** in March. All boat shows feature both new and brokerage (pre-owned) boats. Attendees will be able to see everything from 16 ft flats boats to 200 ft mega yachts.

The Fort Lauderdale International Boat Show is the largest show in the area, and a short drive from the Palm Beaches. It runs Thursday to Monday, with VIP day that first Thursday. While the tickets may be more expensive for the VIP day, it's usually the best day to attend, according to local boat experts. The other best day to attend the show is Monday, when the best boat deals can be made.

The nearby Yachts Miami Beach Show in February takes place along the popular Collins Avenue and features mostly glitzy mega-yachts. The show, which runs Thursday to Monday, is free of charge and typically draws a large international crowd. The separate Miami International Beach Show also takes place around the same time and features mostly new boat builds.

Source: Discover the Palm Beaches
The Palm Beach International Boat Show

Our own Palm Beach International Boat Show attracts thousands of people to its boat exhibitions each year, but feels more manageable than its other boat show counterparts.

7 Insider Tips for Attending a Boat Show

by Audrey Bird,
Director of Events for United Yacht Sales

1. If you are a serious buyer, go Thursday, Friday or Monday. The boat show will be less crowded—as Saturday and Sunday are known for just having "lookers" (a lot of them).

2. Don't bring strollers! These are docks with a lot of people. Be considerate.

3. For clothing, wear easy to remove shoes. Almost all boats are going to require you to take off your shoes in order to board. Make it easy on yourself. Also, dress nicely. Men—no t-shirts or boardshorts. Ladies—no stilettos.

You have no idea how many women we see get their heels stuck and fall. You'll also be climbing all over a boat, so I would advise against wearing a short dress.

4. Splurge for VIP Valet parking especially during the Miami show. Parking is a huge issue with every show and this just takes the headache out of it.

5. Many mega-yachts will not let you onboard—they are for serious buyers only. You have to register for most all mega-yachts and new builds to board.

6. Have an email address on-hand that you use for junk emails. You'll end up giving out your email over 20 times during a show when you register.

7. If possible, walk around with your broker during the show. Your broker can get you tickets, access to yachts, party invites, and more.

License and Registration

Once you've purchased a boat, you have 30 days to register the vessel at the county tax collector's office. For more information on registering your boat, visit www.DMV.org. Those born after January 1, 1988, whose boat is powered by 10 horsepower or greater must pass a boating safety course and obtain a Boating Safety Education ID Card. For more information, visit the **Florida Fish and Wildlife Conservation Commission** website at www.myfwc.com.

Boat Clubs, Rentals, and Charters

Why buy when you can rent? If you're looking for a hassle-free alternative to boat ownership, I strongly recommend joining a nearby boat club. You will get all the benefits of enjoying a boat without having to pay for the insurance, storage, and upkeep. From the **Palm Beach Boat Club** to **Jupiter Inlet Boat Rentals**, there are numerous clubs and boat rental companies in the Palm Beach area. At places like **Blue Heron Fishing** and **Sailfish Marina**, you can also charter a fishing boat for the day.

Beaches and Parks

Life's a beach for Palm Beach residents. With our cerulean ocean and golden shores, each beach offers a unique retreat and an ideal backdrop for Palm Beachers. For a quiet, laid-back place to stick your toes in the sand, I recommend checking out **Gulfstream Park** near Briny Breezes, **South Beach Park** in Boca Raton, **R.G. Kreusler Park** in Palm Beach, and **Ocean Ridge Hammock Park** in Boynton Beach (located near the Boynton Beach Park).

For serene and nature-filled surroundings replete with outdoor activities, explore **John D. MacArthur State Park,** one of Palm Beach County's best treasures. Located on a barrier island, this sandy haven offers two miles of beach, a shallow estuary, wildlife, and rental kayaks. Visitors can canoe, fish, birdwatch, swim, surf, snorkel, and, of course, relax in one of the most lush parks in the county.

**Source: Carl Dawson of LivingExposure and the
Delray Beach Downtown Development Authority**

Source: Discover the Palm Beaches
Lake Worth Beach

If you're looking for a high-energy beach near shops and restaurants, spend the day at the always-lively **Delray Municipal Beach**. The beach is often buzzing with activity, offering plush cabanas and beach chairs for rent as well as watersports activities. Restaurants like the Sandbar, Caffe Luna Rosa, and Boston's on the Beach are also right across the street. Other vibrant beaches include **Palm Beach Municipal Beach**, which is always filled with sunbathers and joggers during the season; and **Lake Worth Municipal Beach**, with its newly renovated Lake Worth Casino Building oceanfront complex. If you live in South County and are looking for a vivacious beach scene, it's worth paying a visit to **Deerfield Beach**, located just south of Boca Raton. The beach, while not technically in Palm Beach County, provides a lively atmosphere with nearby restaurants and shopping boutiques.

**Source: Carl Dawson of LivingExposure and the
Delray Beach Downtown Development Authority
Early morning yoga in the Palm Beaches**

Family Friendly

If you're looking for a kid-friendly beach complete with outdoors showers, clean restrooms, playgrounds, and picnic tables, I suggest heading to Boca Raton's **Spanish River Park**. The park offers everything mentioned above, as well as birdwatching, hiking trails, and saltwater fishing. Other family friendly beaches include **Boynton Beach's Oceanfront Park**; **Carlin Beach** in Jupiter, which also has an amphitheater, picnic pavilions, and tennis courts; and **Red Reef Park** in Boca Raton, which offers great snorkeling and fishing.

For a fun day with friends and family, boat on up to the popular **Jupiter Sandbar**, located in the Jupiter-Tequesta area of the county. The sandbar tends to draw lots of people during weekend afternoons, and is a picturesque spot to picnic and soak up the rays on a warm summer (or winter) day.

A trip out to the famous **Peanut Island Park** is also a must. The enchanting island is home to President Kennedy's Cold-War era shelter. It's also a great place to fish, swim, snorkel, camp, and picnic. The island provides boat docking facilities and restrooms as well.

Fishing and Snorkeling

Palm Beach County offers some of the best fishing anywhere around. Thanks to the warm waters of the Gulf Stream, there's plenty of wahoo, mackerel, bluefish, shark, snook, grouper, snapper, sailfish, swordfish, dolphin, and the occasional marlin available offshore throughout the year. In our freshwater lakes and rivers, fishermen reel in a bevy of catfish, sunfish, and largemouth bass.

Unless you are a child or a senior citizen, you will be required to obtain a freshwater fishing license or a saltwater fishing license—depending on where you plan to fish. A resident recreational saltwater fishing license covers fishing from the shore, a dock, a jetty, and a boat. You can get more information about this license on the **Florida Fish and Wildlife Conservation Commission** website at www.myfwc.com. You can learn more about our best shores, piers, and jetties from which to fish, on **Palm Beach County's website** at www.pbcgov.com.

For saltwater fishing, you can't beat **Juno Beach Park Pier**, **South Inlet Park** in Boca Raton or **Ocean Inlet Park** in Boynton Beach. Tip: these three beaches also provide excellent snorkeling.

**Source: Dana McMahon
The Juno Beach Fishing Pier**

For more snorkeling action, I recommend spending the day at **Ocean Reef Park** in Singer Island or at **Phil Foster Park's** snorkeling trail in Riviera Beach. Many beaches in Palm Beach County require divers and snorkelers to have dive flags visible at all times. So, make sure to check the beach's details before venturing out.

Diving

Our beaches are fantastic, but what lies beyond them is no less spectacular. The Gulf Stream that flows through our ocean waters is accompanied by hundreds of colorful sea creatures, making our scuba diving adventures all the more worthwhile. According to the **Palm Beach Diving Association**, the Palm Beaches' coastline can be split into four sections characterized by different inlets. These include: Jupiter Inlet, Lake Worth Inlet, Boynton Inlet, and Boca Inlet. From here, you can visit some of the best diving spots in the world. www.divepbc.com

Source: Discover the Palm Beaches

I recommend exploring underneath the **Blue Heron Bridge**, where you'll find artificial reefs bursting with colorful marine life. Just a mile off-shore from The Breakers in Palm Beach, scuba divers can also "drift dive" along **The Breakers Reef**. This site provides another fantastic background for tropical fish, turtles, sharks, and even humpback whales.

Dog Parks and Pet-Friendly Beaches

In addition to having numerous pet-friendly housing options, hotels, and restaurants, Palm Beach County also has the top-rated dog-friendly beach in the state and several quality dog parks. You can let your furball off his leash at **Dog Park at Lake Ida** in Delray Beach, **Canine Cove** in Boca Raton, and **Pooch Pines** in West Palm Beach. While dogs are allowed in most county parks, they're only currently allowed off-leash on one beach, **Jupiter Beach**. The beach, which happens to be one of the best dog-friendly beaches in Florida, allows pups to roam freely on certain sections of the shore.

Wildlife

Source: Discover the Palm Beaches

Getting in touch with nature is a walk in the park here in Palm Beach County. With the Florida Everglades' grassy rivers located right in our backyards, along with numerous hiking trails, lagoons, beaches, and waterways, it's easy to get in touch with South Florida's natural surroundings. While meandering through the scenic Loxahatchee River, located in the 260 square-mile **Arthur R. Marshall Loxahatchee National Wildlife Refuge**, visitors may see blue herons, osprey, egrets, American alligators, great-horned owls, American bald eagles, and Florida panthers.

Connecting to the Loxahatchee River, Intracoastal Waterway, and Jupiter Inlet are the **Jupiter Waterway Trails**, a great place for boating, snorkeling, paddle boarding, and kayaking. You'll find plenty of hiking, bird-watching, lush vegetation, and exotic wildlife as well. In Juno Beach, residents can visit the sea turtle world of the **Loggerhead Marinelife Center**. The non-profit and ocean conservation facility features live sea turtles and various sea creatures, special exhibits, educational programs, and a state-of-the-art full service veterinary hospital.

Just west of Palm Beach Gardens and Jupiter lies the expansive **J.W. Corbett Wildlife Area**. A popular place to hunt, this lush ecosystem is home to white-tailed deer and turkey, as well as the endangered red-cockaded woodpecker, endangered snail kite, bobcats, hawks, herons, and numerous other wildlife.

West of Delray Beach, check out the **Wakodahatchee Wetlands** for an up-close look at 140 different species of birds. Locals will tell you that the best times to see the birds are mornings and evenings during the winter months. **The Palm Beach Zoo** and **Lion Country Safari**, both located in West Palm Beach, are other popular attractions for families.

Tennis

Every year, the **Delray Beach Open** takes over our local Delray Beach Tennis Center. The 10-day event features top-ranked international players in the ATP Champions Cup and the ATP World Tour. The winter event attracts over 50,000 spectators to Delray Beach. For tickets and more information, check out www.yellowtennisball.com.

You can also grab a racket and head to one of Palm Beach County's 1,000-plus tennis courts. Throughout the county you'll find both private and public tennis courts, offering everything from classes and clinics to camps and tournaments. Adult tennis leagues are available for every skill level as well. Many condo communities and country club communities also offer tennis court facilities on the grounds.

Polo and Elite Equestrian Sports

I highly recommend venturing out to Wellington's International Polo Club to experience your own sunhat-wearing, divot-stomping, champagne-sipping "Pretty Woman" moment. Polo, known as the "Sport of Kings," dominates the Palm Beach social calendar during the season and is a must-do for all residents. Here's a little information on one of our county's most popular and most elite sporting events.

High-Goal Polo and Elite Equestrian Sports

by Enid Atwater

From January to April, the equestrian region of the Palm Beaches, known as Wellington, is the epicenter of the horse world. The most elite polo players in the world fiercely compete head-to-head on the field, with the balmy South Florida weather providing an exquisite backdrop at the premier polo facility, the International Polo Club Palm Beach (IPC). The glamorous social scene surrounding  the sport includes international jet-setters, corporate giants, celebrities, and trendsetting fashionistas. Exquisite hospitality options at IPC such as the Veuve Clicquot Champagne Lounge, the Lilly Pulitzer Patio, and the exclusive Coco Polo Lounge feature a lavish Sunday brunch for upscale spectators seeking the quintessential Palm Beach experience.

Three of the most prestigious tournaments in the United States, the C.V. Whitney Cup, the USPA Gold Cup®, and the U.S. Open Polo Championship®, are played at IPC annually, with the added caché of luxury brand sponsors supporting the affluent sporting events.

Polo matches are open to the public and weekday matches have no admission fee. Sunday tournament matches require reservations and ticketing. The chic facility offers a wide range of viewing options that include stadium seating, tailgating, and field-side champagne brunch at one of the hospitality venues, along with private member and sponsor boxes. More than 170,000 spectators are accommodated annually at IPC. The club is open for special events, weddings, and corporate entertaining year-round. For information, reservations, and ticketing, visit www.internationalpoloclub.com or call 561.282.5334.

Source: Lila Photo

The Palm Beach International Equestrian Center in Wellington hosts 12 weeks of all things equestrian, from the horse dance ballet of dressage to the Grand Prix show jumpers and hunter disciplines. Competitors take to the ring at one of the largest horse shows in America, the Winter Equestrian Festival (WEF) that runs from January through April.

The winter equestrian season in the Palm Beaches pumps more than $200 million into the local economy, and attracts polo players, equestrian athletes, grooms, trainers, and visitors from all 50 states, and more than 33 countries. It is estimated that close to 15,000 horses make Palm Beach their home during the posh Palm Beach winter season. For more information on WEF, please visit pbiec.coth.com or call 561.793.5867.

A fifth-generation Floridian, and life-long resident of the Palm Beaches, Enid Atwater is a travel and lifestyle publicist representing A-list clients in the Palm Beach area. She previously served as the Vice-President of Corporate Communications for Discover the Palm Beaches, the official tourism agency of Palm Beach County, FL, overseeing national and international public relations and strategic marketing initiatives.

Golf

It's tee time all the time here in the Palm Beaches. Our county is home to the PGA headquarters and host to the celebrated **PGA Tour's Honda Classic**. With 160 public and private golf courses to explore and ideal temperatures year-round, our county is undoubtedly the golf capital of the world.

Those looking for an affordable golf experience will find it at one of our many public golf courses. Rates range anywhere from $10 to $80 per round depending on when and where you want to play. Tee times for the majority of these public courses can be booked online. Membership-based private golf clubs in the Palm Beach area are considerably more expensive. Expect to pay a membership fee of $450 to $25,000 plus annual dues.

Golf Lessons

For those looking to learn or improve their golf swing, I recommend checking out the first-rate classes and clinics taught at **The John Prince Golf Learning Center** in Lake Worth, **The John Webster Golf Academy** at The Breakers in Palm Beach, or the **PGA National Golf Academy** in Palm Beach Gardens. There are also numerous golf academies and golf schools throughout the county for players of all skill levels.

Popular Golf Courses

Red Reef Executive Golf Course, located in East Boca Raton, offers nine holes with sweeping views of the Intracoastal Waterway and the Atlantic Ocean. Further west in Boca Raton, the 27-hole **Osprey Point Golf Course** boasts plenty of verdure and beautiful surroundings, having been named an Audubon International Certified Classic Sanctuary. In the neighboring town of Delray Beach, golfers can explore **The Seagate Country Club**, a world-renowned golf course available to members and Seagate Hotel guests.

Further north in West Palm Beach, lies the **Okeeheelee Golf Course**. This golf course provides 27 holes, three combination courses, and a stunning view of Clear Lake. The historic **West Palm Beach Golf Course** offers a charming 18-hole, par-72 golf course, and also happens to be a former PGA Tour site.

Source: Discover the Palm Beaches
PGA National's gorgeous golf courses

Farther west lies the famous **Ibis Golf and Country Club**. Its private, membership-only golf courses were designed by golf legend Jack Nicklaus and his family. One of the courses was even named "the Most Women-Friendly Course in America" by *Golf for Women* magazine. In Palm Beach, **The Breakers Ocean Golf Course** offers golfers an 18-hole paradise. Nearby lies the hotel's other golf course: the scenic 18-hole **Breakers Rees Jones Course**. Admission to these courses, however, is limited to hotel guests and members.

For the avid golfer, I certainly recommend checking out Palm Beach Gardens' famous **PGA National**, with its five green courses: The Champion, The Fazio, The Squire, The Palmer, and The Estate. Up in Jupiter, the public course at the **Abacoa Golf Club** is a popular spot for locals. Famous courses in the Jupiter area include **The Bear's Club** and the exclusive **Medalist Golf Club** in Hobe Sound, which both boast numerous PGA Tour and LPGA members.

Croquet

West Palm Beach is home to the world's largest croquet facility in the world. **The National Croquet Center** covers four acres of beautiful lawns and includes a large clubhouse for parties and events. Lessons and membership opportunities are available.

Outdoor Festivals

In Palm Beach County, everything is better outdoors—including festivals. The area's oldest and largest outdoor event, the **South Florida Fair**, takes over in the winter with rides, games, and entertainment. Other landmark outdoor festivals include: the **Delray Affair**, the multiple **Holiday Boat Parades**, **4th on Flagler**, **PrideFest**, **SunFest**, the **Delray Beach Garlic Festival**, and **MoonFest**. Throughout the year, residents can also enjoy nights downtown at West Palm Beach's **Screen on the Green** event, as well as **Clematis by Night** and **Sunday on the Waterfront**.

Source: Discover the Palm Beaches
SunFest in West Palm Beach is Florida's largest waterfront music and art festival

Spring Training

Good news for baseball fans—Palm Beach County hosts the Miami Marlins and the St. Louis Cardinals for their annual spring training at the **Roger Dean Stadium** in Jupiter. Two other major league teams, the Houston Astros and Washington Nationals, will soon begin their spring training in Palm Beach County as well. The teams recently signed a deal to begin their spring training in West Palm Beach, starting February 2017.

CHAPTER FIVE

SHOPPING AND DINING

"Style isn't just about what you wear, it's about how you live."
—Lilly Pulitzer, iconic Palm Beach fashion designer and socialite

Source: Palm Beach Lately and South Moon Photography
Sisters and co-founders of Palm Beach Lately, Beth Aschenbach and Danielle Norcross, offer readers a peek inside the modern-day Palm Beach lifestyle.

Palm Beach County is a top destination for retail therapy and good eats. The area offers something for everyone—with dining and shopping hotspots that fit all budgets. It's an eclectic mix of luxury boutiques and thrifty consignment stores. Our dining landscape is unlimited too. Whatever you have a taste for; you'll more than likely find it here in the Palm Beaches.

Fashion and Style

Palm Beach Style Icon Lilly Pulitzer

You can't discuss style in Palm Beach County without touching on our most celebrated fashion icon: Lilly Pulitzer. The genesis of her legendary fashion empire began with a simple yet serendipitous orange juice spill. In an attempt to camouflage the stains, the twenty-something socialite created the famous patterned shift dress while working at her husband's Palm Beach juice stand. The rest—as you know—is history.

"Jackie Kennedy wore one of my dresses—it was made from kitchen curtain material—and people went crazy."– Lilly Pulitzer

Today, there's no doubt that Lilly Pulitzer's perfectly preppy prints, with their flamingo pinks and sunny yellows, have become synonymous with the island's signature look. From the sidewalks of Worth Avenue to the philanthropic American Red Cross Beach Bash, you're sure to see locals donning their best Lilly Pulitzer-inspired looks around town.

Staying Cool

Of course, don't assume everyone in Palm Beach County wears head-to-toe Lilly Pulitzer these days. Thanks to our home's diverse population and wide-array of shopping options, you'll find residents donning every kind of designer name under the warm sun. Nevertheless, there are several uniform rules to live by when it comes to dressing for the Florida heat.

- First, stick with lightweight fabrics like cotton, linen, or seersucker. These breathable fabrics absorb sweat and moisture, allowing faster evaporation so that you stay dry. To avoid sweating buckets, I recommend staying away from synthetic fibers like rayon and polyester.

- Second, stick to light-colored clothing, especially if you're planning to stay outside for a long period of time. Whites and neutrals are the key to staying somewhat cool. Black is a no-no in the hot sun.

- Finally, hats are never a bad idea in the Palm Beaches. Whether you prefer a ball cap or a wide-brimmed sun hat, protecting your face and head should be a top priority.

Style

Dressing in Palm Beach County is all about keeping it casual, comfortable, and chic. You'll see both locals and visitors decked out in everything from sun dresses and lightweight tunics to linen tops and cashmere sweaters. Expect to see seasonal residents sporting resort-casual wear, while locals tend to stick with the season's trends.

Source: Carl Dawson of LivingExposure and the Delray Beach Downtown Development Authority Dressing for Palm Beach

Of course, on the island of Palm Beach there is often an implied preppy dress code. For men, this consists of: country club-approved golf shirts; sport coats and blazers; loafers, boat shoes, or Stubbs & Wootton slippers—no socks; preppy button downs, and Smathers and Branson needlepoint belts.

For women: Lilly Pulitzer-inspired sun dresses and colorful silk blouses; statement jewelry; breezy cover-ups; classic J.McLaughlin tops; white jeans; Jack Rogers sandals, sweaters tied around the shoulders; and wide-brimmed sun hats. You'll also see local ladies donning brands like the Island Company and Calypso St. Barth, as well as plenty of bespoke accessories.

Locals in other parts of the county, however, don't always stick with the resort casual look. Anything below 70 degrees is considered cold by residents, so expect to see locals in booties and light jackets during the less balmy winter months. Thanks to the occasional 45 degree "cold snap," you will need to keep your winter garb handy. Though most restaurants provide heat lamps on their patios, it's always a good idea to to bring along a warm wrap or sweater.

Source: Carl Dawson of LivingExposure and the Delray Beach Downtown Development Authority
A glimpse inside Delray Beach Fashion Week

For those used to the big city-fast-paced-suited up lifestyle, prepare to change your tune. Here in South Florida, everything moves at a slower pace. Unless you work in finance or are headed to a dressy social event, a suit and tie will not be your norm. Jeans, khakis, cotton shifts, and lightweight shirts will be perfectly acceptable in most settings. Men may need a sports coat or polo shirt for nicer restaurants in Palm Beach, however.

Now that you have a better idea of how to build your Palm Beach wardrobe, here's where you can find it.

Main Shopping Hubs in the County

City Place – www.cityplace.com – Located in the heart of West Palm Beach, City Place offers open-air shopping at over 100 different stores, dining, and entertainment. Shops include Anthropologie, H&M, Lucky Brand, and Tommy Bahama, among others.

Downtown at the Gardens – www.downtownatthegardens.com – This pedestrian-friendly shopping experience in Palm Beach Gardens is all about enjoying the outdoors while perusing charming shops, like Sur La Table and Swoozies. The shopping center also offers top-notch dining, a Whole Foods Market, and a wooden carousel.

The Gardens Mall – www.thegardensmall.com – The Gardens Mall is an upscale, two-story, enclosed shopping mall with skylights and grand architectural appointments in Palm Beach Gardens, Florida. Its anchors are Macy's, Sears, Bloomingdale's, Nordstrom, and Saks Fifth Avenue, and it features more than 160 well-known international and national retailers, specialty shops, and restaurants.

Source: The Gardens Mall

Legacy Place – www.shoplegacyplace.com – Another Palm Beach Gardens shopping option, Legacy Place provides locals with access to more than 40 retail stores and restaurants. Shops range from Best Buy and Loehmann's to home decor and pet stores.

The Mall at Wellington Green – www.shopwellingtongreen.com – The Mall at Wellington Green is an excellent shopping mecca. This Mediterranean-style enclosed mall features over 160 shops, including anchor retailers like Dillard's, Nordstrom, Macy's, and JCPenney.

Mizner Park – www.miznerpark.com – Whether you're looking for clothes and home decor or catching a movie or concert, Mizner Park has it all. This Boca Raton shopping center features an outdoor amphitheater, first-class shopping, and an art museum. Mizner Park also features a bevy of restaurants and bars for cocktails and lite bites.

Source: Dana McMahon
Mizner Park

Palm Beach Outlets – www.palmbeachoutlets.com – For those looking for a grand shopping outlet experience, the recently opened Palm Beach Outlets is your best bet. Located in West Palm Beach, the center offers over 100 different outlets, including Nordstrom Rack, Steve Madden, and a non-stop list of recognizable retailers and brands.

Town Center Mall – www.simon.com/mall/town-center-at-boca-raton – The massive indoor mall, located along Glades Road, is a year-round go-to for residents. It is packed all the time—for shopping and dining, and features a wide-array of popular retailers—from Bloomingdales and Neiman Marcus to Pottery Barn and Crate & Barrel.

Worth Avenue – www.worth-avenue.com – Perhaps the most famous shopping district in the country, Palm Beach's legendary Worth Avenue, is dotted with high-end retailers, designer fashion, antiques, jewelry, and top-notch dining. Worth Avenue was also included in *USA Today's* "10 Most Iconic Streets" list. Don't forget to explore the many vias off Worth Avenue, as there are numerous boutiques and restaurants tucked away in these picturesque nooks.

In addition to Worth Avenue, the entire island of Palm Beach is considered a top shopping destination in its own right. In fact, the ritzy isle was even voted as one of the top-five places to shop in the country by readers of *Conde Nast Traveler*.

The Haute Life: Where to Shop in Palm Beach

by Sally Shorr

Known as the "Rodeo Drive of the East Coast," Worth Avenue is a Shangri-La of high-end fashion houses and glamorous boutiques, which make their home along the street's charming vias. Feel like exploring? Here are five boutiques to get lost in right now.

Start your sartorial sojourn with a trip to **Island Bee** (*261 Royal Poinciana Way*). Owner Nick Coniglio's vegan café features house-made organic juices, fruit smoothies, and healthy fare. Splurge: The eatery also stocks handmade jewelry by local gemologist Allegra Fanjul.

High-octane beach chic is on display at **Tomas Maier** (*38 Via Mizner*). Nestled in a Bougainvillea-covered courtyard, Bottega Veneta's creative director likes to complement a bronze glow with edgy, metallic swimsuits, ethereal tunics, and arm-candy python purses. Splurge: Vibrant silk colorblock shift dresses are perfect for sipping cocktails at Café Boulud.

Palm Beach pit stop, **Barzina** (*66 Via Mizner*) is "a place to lose yourself only to find yourself," says owner Gretchen Bentley. The 600-square-foot treasure box bursts with one-of-a-kind furniture, home goods, and fashions from across the globe. Decorate the manse with an 18th-century wood-carved Buddha from Thailand or stock up on blackamoor table linens. Splurge: Start your own zoo with quirky wire monkeys from London.

Parisians and Palm Beachers flock to **Style Paris** (*337 Worth Avenue*), a French imbued outpost that specializes in bespoke silhouettes. Owner and designer Susan Sutherland designs each piece, from pea coats to ball gowns, and sources her fabrics from Loro Piana, Dormeuil, and Bucol. Splurge: Voltige Bis' off-the-shoulder linen dresses are equal parts gamine and femme fatale.

Play shoe designer at **Via Capri, 34** (*323 Worth Avenue*), a tiny boutique that specializes in custom Italian footwear. Pick a silhouette, leather preference, and adornments like Swarovski crystals and precious stones. Splurge: Any of Francesco Pasta's bling encrusted kicks make perfect companions for a Sunday brunch at The Breakers.

A public relations manager at Venue Marketing Group, Sally Shorr has more than 15 years of experience in public relations, TV, and journalism. Recently, Sally exchanged the concrete jungle of Chicago for the tropical beaches of West Palm Beach, where she is obsessed with the eclectic food and fashion scene.

Antique and Furniture Consignment Shopping

Decorators, designers, and collectors from all over the world flock to Palm Beach County for the area's wide selection of consignment stores and antique shops.

For upscale and unique finds, I recommend browsing Palm Beach County's fabulous **Antique Row**, where "antiquing" is practically a sport. The district has been lauded as one of the best shopping areas in the country by publications like *The New York Times*, *House Beautiful*, and *Architectural Digest*. Located along Dixie Highway in West Palm Beach, Antique Row features over 40 antique shops and boutiques—many offering luxury and rare antique finds, as well as Mid-century modern and glamorous Hollywood Regency style furnishings. Check out www.westpalmbeachantiques.com for a more in-depth overview of the district.

I also recommend attending **Evening on Antique Row**, hosted by the Young Friends of the Historical Society of Palm Beach County in partnership with the Antique Row Association. The street festival brings "the Row" to life with live music, entertainment and games, cocktails, food trucks, and luxe shopping. Attendees can explore area shops, which stay open late, with collections of 17th to 20th century antiques, decorative arts, period furnishings, fine art, and design services.

Source: Capehart Photography
Evening on Antique Row

The funky and eclectic **Northwood Village** also makes for a delightful vintage-filled shopping day in West Palm Beach. The historic area hosts an **Art & Wine Promenade** event on the last Friday of every month, giving attendees a chance to meet local artists and to shop the boutiques. As you peruse the neighborhood, I recommend checking out stores like **Gardenhouse**, a vintage indoor-outdoor furniture store, and **Circa Who**, a high-end furniture resale shop bursting with Palm Beach flair, all lacquered in bright white, coral, and turquoise. These stores are the go-to shops for a serious decor splurge and decor inspiration.

For those looking to save a dime, I suggest hunting through the many furniture consignment stores and antique shops located south of West Palm Beach along Route 1. They are everywhere. My personal favorites include the rattan and faux bamboo-filled **Nest** shop in Delray Beach and the tropical vintage-filled **Coconut Consignment Company** in downtown Boca Raton. These top-notch consignment store prices are generally very reasonable.

Groceries

In Palm Beach County, you'll never be without a grocery store nearby. The area is practically inundated with **Publix Super Markets**. The popular Florida-based supermarket chain is one of the 10 largest-volume supermarkets in the country, offering a wide selection of produce, meats, and seafood. For low-cost groceries, you'll find several **Trader Joe's** locations throughout Palm Beach County, including in Delray Beach, Boca Raton, Wellington, and Palm Beach Gardens. Upscale grocery store, **The Fresh Market**, offers specialty foods and plenty of organic options. The supermarkets are located in Boca Raton, Delray Beach, Jupiter, and Wellington. In addition to these grocery stores, the region is also dotted with several **Whole Foods Markets**. The organic grocery store has locations in Boca Raton, Wellington, West Palm Beach, and Palm Beach Gardens.

Farmers Markets

Source: Palm Beach Lately and South Moon Photography
Palm Beach Lately co-founders enjoy a Saturday morning
at the Green Market in West Palm Beach.

You can't beat our locally-grown produce here in Florida. Our state produces everything from oranges and strawberries to sweet corn and tomatoes. According to the Florida Department of Agriculture, Florida accounts for 63% of total U.S. citrus production and ranks second for value of vegetable production. Expect to see a medley of fruits and vegetables at your local farmers markets, as well as a wide selection of quality artisanal products. Here are the can't-miss farmers markets around the county.

North County

Jupiter

Green Market at Abacoa – Open from September to April, 9 a.m. to 1 p.m. on Saturdays

Riverwalk Green & Artisan Market – Open year-round, 10 a.m. to 2 p.m. on Sundays

Jupiter's Farmers Market at Harbourside Place – Open from December to April, 9 a.m. to 2 p.m. on Sundays

Tequesta

Green Market – Open from October to April, 9 a.m. to 1 p.m. on the third Saturday of the month.

Royal Palm Beach

Green Market and Bazaar – Open from October to April, 9 a.m. to 1 p.m. on Sundays

Palm Beach Gardens

Gardens Green Market – Open year-round, 8 a.m. to 1 p.m. on Sundays

Central County

West Palm Beach

Green Market in downtown West Palm Beach – Open from October to May, 9 a.m. to 1 p.m. on Saturdays

Wellington

Green Market – Open from October to April, 9 a.m. to 1 p.m. on Saturdays

Lake Worth

Farmers Market – Open from October to April, 9 a.m. to 2 p.m. on Saturdays

South County

Boca Raton

Green Market – Open from October to May, 8 a.m. to 1 p.m. on Saturdays

West Boca Raton

Mega Green Market – Open year-round, 8:30 a.m. to 2 p.m. on Saturdays

Delray Beach

Green Market – Open from October to May, 9 a.m. to 2 p.m. on Saturdays

To see when specific fruits and vegetables are in season, I recommend checking out the **Florida Department of Agriculture and Consumer Services'** "Crops in Season" list at www.freshfromflorida.com.

Dining

Source: Discover the Palm Beaches
Guanabanas in Jupiter

A Burgeoning Culinary Landscape

At first, newcomers may not realize just how many *excellent* restaurants we have in Palm Beach County. The fresh seafood is scrumptious, the Cuban coffee is hot, the craft cocktails are impeccable. If you're a foodie, you too will be thrilled with the Palm Beaches' palate pleasing eateries. Here are some of the area's staple restaurants and favorite dining neighborhoods.

In North County, locals frequent the hopping waterfront restaurant **Guanabanas** for the fruity tiki drinks and lush ambience. Also in Jupiter, **Square Grouper** is a popular choice. The marina bar offers stunning views of the Jupiter Lighthouse, ice cold Coronas, and live music. **Lazy Loggerhead Cafe** and **Hog Snapper** both offer beach shack favorites like dolphin sandwiches and shellfish appetizers. Other popular watering holes in this area include: **U-Tiki, Jetty's, Schooner's, 2 Vinez, Leftovers Cafe, Oceana Coffee, The Food Shack, Thirsty Turtle, Cafe Chardonnay, Coolinary Cafe,** and **Christopher's Kitchen.** For more top-notch Jupiter and Palm Beach Gardens restaurants, check out the dining options in Harbourside Place, in PGA Commons, and along PGA Boulevard.

In Central County, Palm Beach's iconic restaurants such as **Cafe Boulud, Ta-boo, Cafe L'Europe,** and **Chez Jean-Pierre** offer a dose of timeless Palm Beach ambience and first-rate dining. James Beard nominated chef and restaurateur Clay Conley provides locals with innovative fare at his lauded upscale-casual spots—**Buccan** and **Imoto** in Palm Beach, and **Grato** in West Palm Beach's Flamingo Park neighborhood. Other top tables in Central County include the Palm Beach staple restaurants **Meat Market, Flagler Steakhouse, HMF at The Breakers,** and **Nick & Johnnie's.**

Cross the bridge into West Palm Beach and you'll find an up-and-coming food scene bursting with South Florida's best flavors. The city's burgeoning culinary landscape includes City Place eateries and Clematis Street favorites such as **Hullabaloo, Pistache, E.R. Bradley's, Avocado Grill, Rocco's Tacos, Grease Burger Bar,** and **Palm Sugar**. In the funky Northwood Village neighborhood north of Clematis, you'll find local favorites that include **Table 427, O-BO, Cafe Centro,** and **Relish & More**. Farther south of Clematis, the historic Flamingo Park neighborhood lights up with classic restaurants including **Table 26**. Other favorites like **Havana, Darbster, Belle & Maxwell's,** and **La Sirena** line Dixie Highway.

Source: Discover the Palm Beaches
The classic Palm Beach restaurant, Ta-boo, is a must-try on Worth Avenue.

Source: Libby Vision
A look inside James Beard award-nominated Chef Clay Conley's latest venture, Grato.

Hopping nightlife for young professionals can be found along Clematis Street and in City Place—as well as at **Meat Market** and **Cucina Dell' Arte** in Palm Beach. For bottomless Mimosas and Bloody Marys the next day, check out the new poolside brunch with Dj Adam Lipson at the **Hilton West Palm Beach** on Saturdays.

Eat Like a Local in West Palm Beach

by Caitlin Parker

I have never heard anyone say that moving is fun, but getting to know your new digs in West Palm Beach can definitely be an adventure! Here are a few of my favorite eats for cooking at home or dining out—all packed into one weekend.

Source: Dana McMahon

Friday nights are tough after a long work-week, so I make my way over to **Celis Produce** to pick up some locally grown organic produce and cooking supplies for a quiet night in. What they offer changes daily, depending on the season, but every time I go I can't resist the organic local free-range eggs, long grain brown rice, and ripe kiwi. **Celis** also offers free delivery in West Palm Beach, for those looking to stay in over the weekend.

The place to be on a sunny Saturday morning is without a doubt the West Palm Beach **GreenMarket**. Grab yourself a café latte from one of the many vendors, and peruse for locally grown fruits and veggies, flowers, potted herbs, and specialty items like Florida beef jerky, habanero key-lime hot sauce, handcrafted artisan soaps, dog treats, handmade biscotti, cider donuts, cake push pops, and honey from Florida beehives.

Earlier on Saturday nights we often find ourselves at **Morton's Steakhouse's** "Happy Hour," eating scrumptious $8 bites like tuna tacos and filet mignon sliders. And after the crowds have eaten, we head over to **Grato** to find a seat at the open-kitchen bar. We just can't resist the house made bucatini carbonara, brick oven pizzas and wines on tap!

To round out the weekend, you can't go wrong enjoying the Sunday brunch scene at **Lynora's Osteria** on Clematis Street. The brunch features a live DJ, unlimited Bloody Marys, Mimosas, Bellinis, and Peronis, as well as fresh ricotta donuts. My husband would say you need to get their meatball sliders, but my advice is to stay all afternoon and enjoy your bottomless drinks. Cheers!

A self-described "foodie," Caitlin Parker is a young professional living in downtown West Palm Beach. After work, you can find her drinking sauvignon blanc and nibbling on cheese at a number of downtown establishments or strolling around the city with her miniature dachshund, Bailey.

South County's food scene is no less delectable. Waterfront restaurants such as **Two Georges, Banana Boat, Hudson, Deck 84, 50 Ocean, Lucca,** and **Waterstone Bar & Grill** offer stunning views of the Atlantic Ocean and the Intracoastal Waterway right from the dining room.

Delray Beach includes dozens of culinary delights on and off "the Ave." Upscale restaurants such as **32 East, The Grove, Brule, La Cigale,** and **Tramonti** offer everything from fresh seafood and locally-grown ingredients to Mediterranean pasta dishes and high-end wine labels. Nearby, **DaDa** offers an eclectic menu under the stars at their tree-lined patio. Down by the coast, **Boston's on the Beach** has been serving patrons for 35 successful years. The sports bar is a favorite among Boston sports fans.

Other notable restaurants in the area include: **Papa's Tapas, Max's Harvest, The Sundy House, Caffe Martier, The Office, Rocco's Tacos, J&J Seafood Bar, Max's Social House, Park Tavern, Cut 432,** and **City Oyster**. The truth is, the restaurant possibilities in Delray Beach are endless and the quality is unbeatable. Expect to pay big city prices (except during "Happy Hour"), but it's hard to go wrong anywhere in this neighborhood.

Another favorite area for foodies is Boca Raton's Mizner Park. Hotspots in and around the area include **Racks Downtown Eatery, Tanzy, Kapow Noodle Bar,** and **Max's Grill** – among many others.

Other notable restaurants elsewhere in Boca Raton include **The Rebel House, 13 American Table, Arturo's Ristorante, Casa D'Angelo, Henry's,** and **Pavilion Grille.**

Source: Dana McMahon
Two Georges in Boynton Beach

Local Foods

South Florida offers a melting pot of gastronomic delights. For starters, Palm Beach County is known for its local **stone crabs**—typically served with a side of mustard dipping sauce. The stone crab season begins around October and runs through May, providing residents with fresh, succulent claw meat at nearly every seafood-serving eatery in the Palm Beaches. Sidenote: there are quite a few restrictions placed on stone crab fishing in Florida, including the provision that stone crabs must be thrown back into the water after declawing. This allows the crab to continue living and to regrow its claws over time.

Expect to see plenty of **conch fritters, fried gator bites, conch chowder, Florida lobster, peel and eat shrimp,** and every kind of fish imaginable—from **snapper** and **mahi mahi** to **grouper** and **tuna**—on local restaurant menus. Flavors like **mango, coconut,** and **key lime** add sweetness and tang to our seafood dishes, libations, and desserts. Of course, you'll also taste plenty of Caribbean and Cuban influences in our dishes as well. **Cubano sandwiches, fried plantains, jerk chicken, rum cake,** and **Cuban coffee** appear frequently when eating out.

A Hopping Craft Beer Scene

Here in the Palm Beaches, we love a locally-brewed craft beer as much as we love our fancy, white tablecloth dining. Palm Beach County's drinking scene offers a casual sophistication for the most part. In fact, many newcomers don't know that our county has one of the most hopping craft beer scenes you'll find anywhere in Florida.

Tequesta Brewing Co. and its sister establishment, **Twisted Trunk Brewing**, offer residents light IPAs and pilsners in both Tequesta and in Palm Beach Gardens. Other local brews to explore in the area include a Caramel Cream Ale at **Due South Brewing** in Boynton Beach, a Belgian ale from **Barrel of Monks Brewing** in Boca Raton, and a "Screamin' Reels IPA" from **Saltwater Brewery** in Delray Beach. In West Palm Beach, I recommend checking out **The Alchemist**, a gastropub and bar, offering craft beers, wine, and cocktails. If wine is more your speed, I recommend **The Blind Monk**, a chic wine bar with live music every Tuesday in West Palm Beach.

Food Festivals

Here in Palm Beach, we don't just eat food—we celebrate it. Notable foodie festivals to look forward to during the year include: **Palm Beach Food & Wine Fest, Brew at the Zoo Palm Beach, Delray Bacon & Bourbon Fest, Delray Beach Wine and Seafood Festival, Boca Bacchanal,** and of course, our "Restaurant Week," dubbed **Flavor Palm Beach.**

CHAPTER SIX
ARTS AND CULTURE

"Ask anyone with cultural cred and they'll tell you: The arts have never been hotter in South Florida."

— Sun-Sentinel

With its world-class museums, theaters, art galleries, and abundance of homegrown talent, the Palm Beaches is lighting South Florida's arts and culture landscape on fire. In addition to having our own Cultural Council, we're just a hop, skip, and a jump away from Miami's booming arts scene. Here's a look at why this region of the state is the cultural capital of Florida.

Art Districts and Events

In Palm Beach County, there is almost always an art event or special exhibit happening somewhere nearby. If you find yourself in West Palm Beach, I recommend scouting out the **Northwood Village Art Walk**. Guided art tours of the neighborhood are held the second Saturday of every month—although, you can always explore the eclectic art district's boutiques and galleries on your own time. West Palm Beach is also home to the popular contemporary art fair, **ArtPalmBeach**. The event features everything from photography and sculpture exhibits to canvas and art installations.

Artists Alley warehouses in the Pineapple Grove Arts District

Up north in the Jupiter and Juno Beach areas, the **Annual Art Fest by the Sea** takes over the A1A oceanfront every spring. During the winter months, you can also catch the annual **ArtiGras Fine Arts Festival** at Jupiter's Abacoa Town Center.

Farther south, Lake Worth offers an artistic hub worth exploring. Every year, the quirky, artsy city throws the largest "**Street Painting Festival**" in the country, with hundreds of artists using the asphalt streets as their canvas. Lake Worth is also home to multiple art galleries, the **Lake Worth Art League,** the **Lake Worth Art League Outdoor Show,** and the headquarters of the **Cultural Council of Palm Beach County**. Bottom line: there's a lot of art happening in Lake Worth.

The same can be said for sunny Delray Beach. The south county village features the popular **Arts Garage**, which was labeled by the *Sun Sentinel* as a "cultural powerhouse." This arts hub features various musicians, actors, and artists on a regular basis, and is located in the gallery-lined **Pineapple Grove** district. Nearby in Boynton Beach, locals are able to enjoy the city's **Avenue of the Arts** and the **International Kinetic Art Exhibit and Symposium**. The city is well-known as an enclave for artists, with its **Boynton Beach Art District** and monthly **Art Walks**.

**Source: Discover the Palm Beaches
Lake Worth Street Painting Festival**

Farther south, you can get a taste for Boca Raton's vibrant art scene at the **Festival of the Arts BOCA** event at Mizner Park. The 10-day cultural arts event features the best in jazz, film, art, and literature.

Architecture and Design

Florida Architecture and Design Offers Something for Everyone

by Susan Friedman

The Florida lifestyle has all the trappings of a permanent vacation—beginning with resort-style amenities, posh pools and spacious lanais dotted with comfy loungers and fire pits. Tropical palms tower over niches of dense foliage. Design-wise, chic, subtle

patterns, lots of texture and saturated colors are haute for outdoors. Designers need only the water, sky and shore for inspiration.

While having your toes-in-the sand and taking a dip in azure-hued waves is the ultimate postcard moment to experience first-hand—Palm Beach County has so much to offer aside from such traditional musts. Especially for architecture buffs, our diverse landscape exemplifies an enduring history that is as much about culture and lifestyle as it is climate.

Whether you're seeking condos with sky-high views of the Atlantic Ocean or have an urban setting in the thick of dining hotspots and activities in mind—it's true that the architecture of the area will be relevant. And in Palm Beach County, you can select from a broad range of architectural styles certain to match your lifestyle.

Here are just a few noteworthy examples:

Famed architect Addison Mizner reinvented coastal affluence in the 1920's and '30s in Palm Beach. His Italian and Spanish-esque eclectic villas reveal a Mediterranean aesthetic embraced by graceful masonry and multistory facades. To this day, Mizner's legacy remains pivotal to the county's iconic architectural heritage.

Originating in North Florida's rural communities is the classic Cracker house. Designed to provide shelter from the sun, these simple Vernacular houses with wood frames and enormous southern appeal date back to the turn of the 19th century.

In contrast, Key West style homes offer plenty of conch charm. Early settlers used conch shells as building materials. Known for wraparound porches designed to provide shade and wood shutters to let the breezes flow through, these structures embody both Victorian and Bahamian styles, including energy-efficient, heat-deflecting sloping metal roofs.

The Sarasota School of Architecture was a movement that began in the 1940s that brought innovations in cross-ventilation when Florida was in pre-air-conditioning mode. Influential architects Paul Rudolph and Ralph Twitchell constructed modular homes that were harmonious to the environment with oversize sliding glass-doors and jalousie windows.

Whatever your lifestyle and wherever you ultimately choose to kick-off your flip-flops and call home, your options are limitless. From coastal condos to historic bungalows and beyond, Palm Beach County is a playground in more ways than one.

Susan Friedman is a lifestyle journalist whose 25-year career includes writing about interior design, architecture, travel, food and more! The former senior editor of Florida Travel + Life magazine, Susan loves living in sunny south Florida and exploring the next great place to live and play. See her work at: www.susanfriedmanjournalistcopywriter.com

Museums

Good news—when the weather heats up during the summer months, there's still plenty to do inside, including perusing some of the best museums in the country. For starters, West Palm Beach's **Norton Museum of Art** is a must-see. The world-renowned art museum features a permanent collection of 19th and 20th Century artwork, including masterpieces by Georgia O'Keeffe, Matisse, Monet, and Picasso. In addition to special exhibits, the museum also hosts fun events for art buffs, like **"Art After Dark,"** a weekly program that features music, gallery tours, and even, wine tastings.

Just a short car ride away in West Palm Beach lies the **Richard and Pat Johnson Palm Beach County History Museum.** Located inside a restored 1916 Courthouse, the museum is a South Florida history fan's dream come true. Admission is free and inside you'll find state-of-the-art, interactive exhibits that reflect the influence of our county's history and many cultures—from Native Americans to present-day civic and cultural leaders, in 3,000 square feet of permanent gallery space.

Source: Discover the Palm Beaches
The Flagler Museum

Across the Intracoastal Waterway, residents can visit Palm Beach's fantastic **Society of the Four Arts**. This majestic cultural center features an array of lectures, concerts, art exhibits, films, and, of course, some of the most stunning sculpture and botanical gardens you'll see anywhere. It's worth a visit, simply for its beautiful garden oasis. While you're there make sure to smell the Chinese Garden's Ylang-ylang tree, which served as the inspiration for the iconic Chanel No. 5's fragrance.

Another museum on the island worth visiting is the **Flagler Museum**. Located inside the famous Whitehall estate, the museum is a National Historical Landmark that was once owned by Palm Beach's founder, Henry Flagler. Today, the Flagler Museum serves as a venue for some of Palm Beach's most prodigious events and art exhibits. It is also a window into America's glittery Gilded Age.

If you head up to Jupiter, I recommend stopping in at the **Jupiter Inlet Lighthouse Museum**, a historic landmark featuring the waterfront History Museum and climbing tours of the lighthouse. South of West Palm Beach, you can browse Delray Beach's famed **Morikami Museum and Japanese Gardens**. Farther south, you'll find the kid-friendly **Boca Raton Museum of Art**, located in downtown Boca Raton's Mizner Park.

Music and Theater

Whether it's classical ballet or a comedy show, you can enjoy just about any type of performing arts in the Palm Beaches. In West Palm Beach, the **Kravis Center for Performing Arts** offers residents a premier performing arts center, with performances by the Miami City Ballet, Palm Beach Opera, Palm Beach Pops, and much more. The award-winning **Maltz Jupiter Theatre** is another great spot to catch musical productions and concerts, as is Delray Beach's **Crest Theatre** in Old School Square. The **Mizner Park Amphitheater** in Boca Raton provides an outdoor venue for live concerts and events throughout the year. If you're looking to laugh 'till you cry, I suggest catching the improv and stand-up comedy shows at either **Palm Beach Improv**, the **Performing Arts Academy of Jupiter,** or **Sick Puppies Comedy** in Boca Raton.

For live local music, check out **Sunday on the Waterfront** in West Palm Beach. The waterfront concert series takes place on the third Sunday of every month from 4 to 7 p.m. and is free of charge. West Palm's weekly concert series, **Clematis by Night**, takes place every Thursday from 6 to 9 p.m., featuring live music, food, and entertainment. Of course, as a new Palm Beach resident, it's your newcomer duty to attend South Florida's largest waterfront music and art festival, **SunFest**. The concert features more than 50 bands over the course of five days in West Palm Beach.

Source: Discover the Palm Beaches
The Kravis Center for the Performing Arts

Additionally, concert venues worth exploring include Lake Worth's **Bamboo Room**, Boca Raton's **The Funky Biscuit**, and West Palm Beach's popular music venue, **Perfect Vodka Amphitheatre.** You can also catch live music at plenty of bars and restaurants during the weekends. I recommend **Respectable Street** and **Copper Blues** in West Palm Beach; **Johnnie Brown's**, **DaDa**, and the **Colony Hotel & Cabana Club** in Delray Beach; **Square Grouper** in Jupiter; and **The Funky Buddha Lounge** in Boca Raton.

CHAPTER SEVEN

CHOOSING THE RIGHT COMMUNITY

For those set on purchasing a home here, you're in luck. There really is something for everyone in Palm Beach County because the people living here represent every kind of background, lifestyle, and budget imaginable. If you're looking for a vibrant restaurant and nightlife scene, then I recommend settling in West Palm Beach or Delray Beach. If great shopping, golf courses, and tennis courts are on your list of needs, then Palm Beach Gardens or Boca Raton could be a great choice for you. If you're searching for a peaceful seaside town, you'll find it in Juno Beach. If watersports, boating, and golfing are your priority, then Jupiter's many neighborhoods could be a fit for you.

With so many fabulous towns to choose from, house hunting here in Palm Beach County is no easy feat. However, this is—of course—a good problem to have. Here's how to find the right home that fits both your price-point and your lifestyle.

First, decide on a budget. Make sure to check on any HOA fees and membership fees, which in Florida can be notoriously high. These neighborhood association costs are used for landscaping and maintenance for common areas, amenities such as clubhouses, pools, etc., and to keep local buildings up-to-code (such as installing hurricane proof windows) as well as repairing damage from hurricanes, storms, and the like. The closer your home is to the ocean, the more maintenance it will need. Also, make sure to inquire about a building's reserves, in the event of significant repair needs.

Source: Virtual Global Realty

Second, decide what you want and need from a home. Write out the features that are most important to you. A few of the features that my husband and I considered included: proximity to restaurants, commute time, number of bedrooms, and proximity to the beach. By prioritizing what you really need and what you merely want, you'll quickly be able to spot whether a home is a fit or not.

Third, Get the lay of the land by spending time in your top community choices. Go to dinner, hang out in a coffee shop, talk to the locals—get a real feel for the place. It also doesn't hurt to search for real estate online, using websites like Trulia, MLS, and Zillow, to get a sense of what type of real estate is out there and what neighborhoods you'd like to further investigate.

After determining which towns could be a fit, I recommend recruiting a real estate professional to show you around. Getting an in-person driving tour with an expert will give you a much clearer vision of where you want to be.

Finally, keep an open mind about the Palm Beach area. Before my husband and I began our house hunting in-person, we already had ideas of where we wanted to be. Our top-notch realtors, however, opened our eyes to other possibilities in towns we hadn't even considered. That's why it's very important to do your homework and make sure you're hiring the right realtor for the job.

Important Questions to Discuss with Your Realtor

Below is a list of important questions to ask yourself and discuss with your realtor when figuring out where you want to live in the county. Consider it your community checklist. While it's certainly not meant to be the end all, be all of your house hunting decision, it should help to point to you in the right direction.

Questions	Notes
Do I want to be within walking or biking distance to the beach?	Not necessarily
Do I want to live in a rural environment?	NO
Do I need boat storage near my home?	NO
What is my budget (take into account HOA and membership fees)?	$ 2,000/month max
Is it important that I live near a pet-friendly beach or dog park?	No
Is that historic, old Florida charm important to me in a home, or do I prefer modern construction with little updates needed?	newer home
Are schools and a family-friendly environment a factor?	NO
Do I want to live near music and concert venues?	not a priority

Do I want to live closer to the happening scenes in Miami and Fort Lauderdale?	NO
Do I want to live in a peaceful, quiet community?	yes
Is it important that I live very close to Palm Beach International Airport?	NO
Do I want to live in a city with a lot of young professionals, singles, and nightlife?	NO
Is it important that I live in a pedestrian-friendly town?	yes
Is it important that I live near great restaurants and coffee shops?	yes
Do I need a furnished home?	NO
Am I looking for a 55-plus age-restricted community?	Not really
Am I okay with renovating an older home that costs less?	maybe
Do I want to live in a gated community?	yes
Are water activities like swimming, snorkeling, jet skiing, and boating important to me?	no

Renting in Palm Beach County

If you're a Palm Beach County newbie, strongly consider renting the first year—especially if you don't know the area all that well. Renting in the Palm Beaches allows newcomers to get to know the Gold Coast, try it on for size, and ultimately determine where to end up long-term. Rental rates vary from town to town, and greatly depend on proximity to the ocean, surrounding neighborhoods, whether furnished, and special amenities.

The overall average monthly rental rate in Palm Beach County is around $2,800, with a current inventory pushing 40,000 available units. Word to to the wise: Many locals, who also own homes up north, will rent their furnished Palm Beach County homes out for the season or low season. As you're searching online for rentals, make sure to double check whether or not the home is a seasonal rental.

Real Estate Services

As you start your hunt for a realtor or broker, I suggest checking out www.Realtor.com's "Find Realtors" section. I should also note that given the amount of expensive real estate in the Palm Beaches (think: the mega-mansions in Palm Beach, Manalapan, Wellington, Jupiter Island, and Boca Raton), there are quite a few realtors and brokers who deal mostly with the niche luxury real estate market.

CHAPTER EIGHT

BEYOND THE HEDGES: A COMPREHENSIVE GUIDE TO PALM BEACH COUNTY COMMUNITIES

"Hedges are bountiful. No matter how hard-edged or many-layered,
they soothe eyes and ears. On the street, they soften the hard lines and
intersections of asphalt and concrete, of streets and sidewalks, of bald
and barren parking lots...."

– Florida Weekly

Our large county and diverse population can be divided into four distinct sections: North County, Central County, South County, and "the Glades." A total of 38 municipalities exist within the Palm Beaches, but for the sake of this book (and your sanity), I will only be covering some of the most popular places to live. While each of these geographic divisions has its own character, rest assured that they all share Florida's trademark balmy breezes and beautiful backdrops.

The following community snapshots include housing prices, school ratings, demography, and important names to know in the town.

North County

Jupiter

Ranked as one of "America's Happiest Seaside Towns" by *Coastal Living*, this serene community is without a doubt one of the most beautiful and popular places to live in the Palm Beaches. Though Jupiter is just a quick half-hour drive from downtown West Palm Beach, the town feels a million miles away from the hustle and bustle of city living. Roughly 60,000 people live within Jupiter's 21 square miles of land and waterways. The town's most famous attraction is the Jupiter Inlet Lighthouse, which dates back to the 19th century. Jupiter also happens to be one of the most pet-friendly areas in Palm Beach County, with an off-leash dog beach that attracts pet owners from all over the state.

Source: Discover the Palm Beaches
Jupiter Inlet Lighthouse

What Your Money Can Buy: Real estate choices in Jupiter range from well-manicured, golf course communities and beachfront homes to townhouses and upscale condos. With the median home price in Jupiter listed around $469,000, living in Jupiter can be pricier than living in other parts of the county. Then again, Jupiter residents will tell you the quality of life is worth the extra bucks. The average rent for a two-bedroom unit is priced around $2,500 a month. The main residential area in Jupiter is Abacoa, a self-contained community with approximately 6,000 homes. Starter homes in Abacoa begin around $400,000. The area's great schools also make the community a popular choice for families and young couples.

Source: Virtual Global Realty
Admirals Cove is one of Jupiter's finest private gated communities.

Neighbors: With 86 percent of the workforce employed in white-collar jobs, this coastal community skews higher up on the socio-economic spectrum. As you'll find is the case for many Palm Beach County towns, roughly half of Jupiter's residents are seasonal. While the average age in Jupiter is 47, there are plenty of residents of all ages living throughout the town. Celebrities, young professionals, and families all call Jupiter home.

School Report Card: AreaVibes gives Jupiter's schools a score of "A". GreatSchools gives the community schools an overall score of 9 out of 10 (with 10 being the highest). AreaVibes bases their scores on total number of schools, test scores, and student/teacher ratio. GreatSchools ratings are based on local school test results.

Names to Know: Many well-known celebrities have homes in or around Jupiter, including: Tiger Woods, Celine Dion, Kid Rock, Alan Jackson, Michael Jordan, Greg Norman (golfer), and Gary Player (golfer).

Tequesta

Located just north of Jupiter, Tequesta encompasses roughly 5,000 residents in its tiny 2.2 square mile vicinity. These lucky residents can enjoy the waterfront of the Loxahatchee River, the Intracoastal Waterway, as well as the Atlantic Ocean on a daily basis. Like Jupiter, the area's waterways make the village of Tequesta a unique place to live, perfect for folks who love to boat, kayak, paddleboard or just spend time by the water.

What Your Money Can Buy: Tequesta real estate consists of mostly single family homes, waterfront homes, and condos. Relative to other communities, Tequesta's housing inventory tends to be older (developed back in the 1950s and '60s) with fewer clear-cut communities. Older homes can be found in the $300,000 range in Tequesta Pines, however, they'll most likely need to be brought up to code for hurricane protection. Additionally, if a home doesn't fit newer building codes, your home insurance may be higher. Remodeled Tequesta homes could command a price above $500,000. The average rental rate for a two-bedroom unit is priced at $2,000 a month.

Neighbors: Like Jupiter, Tequesta has an interesting mix of year-round and seasonal residents. Due to its pricey waterfront housing on the Loxahatchee River, Tequesta residents include business executives and wealthy retirees. While the Tequesta housing market once attracted blue-collar families looking to escape Jupiter's higher priced communities, it is now being targeted for serious remodeling as more affluent residents move to the area.

School Report Card: AreaVibes gives Tequesta schools a score of "A". GreatSchools doesn't have a score for Tequesta schools, as there is only one private PK-6 school in the town. However, students in Tequesta may be zoned for Jupiter schools.

Names to Know: Burt Reynolds and Joe Namath.

Juno Beach

A sleepy seaside town just south of Jupiter, Juno Beach is an ideal community for those seeking a quiet, beach-centered lifestyle. The tiny beach town is home to 4,000 residents in its 1.9 square miles of pristine coastline. Besides beautiful beaches, Juno Beach also boasts the popular Loggerhead Marinelife Center, a nonprofit education and ocean conservation facility that houses a variety of exhibits, live sea turtles, and other coastal creatures.

Source: Florida Motion Media
Loggerhead Marinelife Center of Juno Beach

What Your Money Can Buy: Real estate in this quiet little town includes waterfront homes, oceanfront condos, and townhomes. The median listing price in Juno Beach is $390,000. The average rental rate for a two-bedroom unit is approximately at $3,400, reflecting tighter inventory and fewer low-end units. One major draw of Juno Beach is that, unlike many other Palm Beach County communities, the town's oceanfront condos are located directly on the beach. In much of Jupiter, for instance, Coastal Highway A1A runs between the beach and condos. The oceanfront land south of Juno Beach is home to the John MacArthur State Park and to several exclusive golf communities, leaving little room for beachfront housing. One caveat: home insurance costs in Juno Beach can be higher due to the close proximity to the water.

Neighbors: Juno Beach's small community tends to draw an older and affluent crowd. It's also an appealing option for boat owners given its proximity to the ocean.

School Report Card: AreaVibes gives Juno Beach schools a score of "A+". GreatSchools doesn't have a score for Juno Beach schools, as there is only one public and private school in the town.

Names to Know: Florida Power and Light Company (headquartered in Juno Beach) and Loggerhead Marinelife Center.

Palm Beach Gardens

Located just 20 minutes north of West Palm Beach, Palm Beach Gardens is a suburban paradise for those looking for top-notch schools, beautiful golf courses, gated communities, and world-class shopping. The city is made up of 54,000 people living throughout its 55.3 square miles. Palm Beach Gardens is best known as a golf haven, serving as the headquarters of the PGA. As you might expect, it is also home to some of the best golf courses in the country, including PGA National Resort's championship golf courses.

Source: Virtual Global Realty
Steeplechase is a popular luxury estate home community in Palm Beach Gardens.

What Your Money Can Buy: When looking at real estate in Palm Beach Gardens, expect to see numerous golf course communities, as well as townhomes, villas, gated communities, and some waterfront homes. The median listing price in Palm Beach Gardens is $429,000. Be aware that many Palm Beach Gardens and Jupiter golf communities require an equity golf membership, which can cost upwards of $100,000 or more. For more affordable living, consider Palm Beach Gardens' townhouse communities such as Trevi at the Garden. Rent prices aren't astronomical in Palm Beach Gardens. Newcomers can find a two-bedroom rental unit for roughly $2,700 a month.

Neighbors: Palm Beach Gardens is a unique mix of upper-class families, golf and tennis enthusiasts, young professionals, and blue-collar workers. The makeup of Palm Beach Gardens is similar to that of Jupiter, except the town is more centered around golf and tennis than water-based activities. The only public beach in Palm Beach Gardens is located at MacArthur State Park.

School Report Card: AreaVibes gives Palm Beach Gardens' schools a score of "A". GreatSchools gives the community schools a score of 7 out of 10.

Names to Know: Serena and Venus Williams, The Professional Golfers' Association of America, John D. MacArthur (visionary and developer of Palm Beach Gardens), and PGA Boulevard.

Other North County communities to consider include: North Palm Beach, Jupiter Inlet Colony, Lake Park, and Riviera Beach/Singer Island.

Central County

Palm Beach

Not all of us can afford to live in a palatial Palm Beach home, but that doesn't mean we can't visit (or dream). Regardless of where you end up living in the county, a trip along Coastal Highway A1A to Palm Beach's hedge-lined "Billionaire's Row" is certainly in order. The "Palm Beach look," namely Mediterranean and Tuscan style architecture, can be attributed to Addison Mizner's vision for the town back in the 1920's. The architect developed many of the island's signature Palm Beach mansions. Located across the water from West Palm Beach, the Palm Beach barrier island has a year-round population of roughly 10,000 residents. I should mention, though, that the island's "season" population comes in around 30,000 people—add tourists to the mix and the island feels much busier during the winter months.

Palm Beach's beautifully landscaped hedges lend privacy to residents.

What Your Money Can Buy: If you're looking to purchase a home in Palm Beach, be prepared to part with millions. Expensive estates encircle the island along the Intracoastal Waterway to the west and the Atlantic Ocean to the east. Just about every home here is located within walking distance of the beach, making the island's interior estates nearly as desirable as its waterfront property. The median listing price in Palm Beach is around $795,000. A waterfront home on the island, however, could start at $3 million—plus considerable carrying costs such as renovations, landscaping, and property taxes. Needless to say, rentals in Palm Beach are priced considerably higher than in other areas of the county. A one-bedroom apartment rental unit on the island will cost you about $3,400 a month, while a two-bedroom rental could cost you upwards of $5,600.

Neighbors: With a median income of roughly $100,000 and an average age of 64, the Palm Beach community is in general, a well-to-do, older crowd. No surprise there. However, no single metric can fully capture the eclectic and interesting mix that makes up Palm Beach's jet set crowd. Residents include: celebrities, artists, novelists, philanthropists, hedge fund managers, trust fund babies, real estate titans, and yes, even Donald Trump's hair.

School Report Card: AreaVibes gives Palm Beach schools a score of "A+". GreatSchools gives the community schools a score of 8 out of 10.

Names to Know: Henry Flagler (founder of Palm Beach), Palm Beach Daily News (also known as "The Shiny Sheet"), Worth Avenue, Mar-A-Lago, Marjorie Merriweather Post (heiress), Addison Mizner, Lilly Pulitzer, Donald Trump, Bernie Madoff, and many *many* more.

West Palm Beach

Source: Discover the Palm Beaches
The West Palm Beach skyline.

With roughly 113,000 residents within its 58.2 square miles, West Palm Beach is the largest city in the county as well as the county seat of the Palm Beaches. Since the '90's, the city of West Palm Beach has undergone dramatic growth and development. What was once an overlooked city playing second fiddle to its ritzy neighbor across the water has now become a vibrant, thriving metropolis in its own right. First-rate restaurants, world-class artists, and exciting nightlife now define this burgeoning city. On any given day in West Palm, you could see residents boating along the Intracoastal Waterway, shopping at CityPlace or brunching at one of Clematis Street's popular restaurants. These activities are, of course, only scratching the surface of everything that West Palm Beach has to offer.

What Your Money Can Buy: For those looking to live in the city center, West Palm Beach has a variety of urban condos and high rise apartments in the downtown area. Living downtown will put you within walking distance and a short trolley ride away from all of the activity happening near CityPlace, Clematis Street, and the waterfront. The average rent for a two-bedroom unit in West Palm Beach is roughly $2,311. If you're interested in living in a city center luxury condo, places like One City Plaza and Two City Plaza are good options. The full service condo buildings are centrally located and include a rooftop pool and gym. Rental prices for a two-bedroom condo range from roughly $2,500 to $4,500. To buy a City Plaza condo will cost you anywhere from $200,000 to upwards of a million or more.

Source: Dana McMahon
CityPlace in West Palm Beach.

Another popular condominium building downtown is The Prado, which features two-bedroom rentals for under $2,000 a month and condos for sale under $200,000. For a condo with a front-seat view of Palm Beach and the Intracoastal Waterway, I recommend also looking at The Trianon building, which typically offers rentals ranging anywhere from $2,500 to $5,000, and condos priced at about half-a-million or more.

All of these downtown condo buildings mentioned above are within walking distance from one another, making it easy to comparison shop. The full-service condominium complexes also offer a wide range of amenities and floor plans.

Single family homes and townhome communities are another popular housing option in West Palm Beach. The median listing price for homes comes in at $224,000. Many of the city's turn-of-the-century single family homes near the Intracoastal Waterway have been remodeled in recent years. Historic neighborhoods like El Cid, Old Northwood, and Flamingo Park are popular communities in West Palm. Single family homes located near the waterfront in El Cid typically cost in the millions. However, just up the street in Flamingo Park, you can find bungalows for around $500,000. Farther north, the Old Northwood Historic District features beautiful craftsman cottages, Spanish-style bungalows, and homes that reflect architect Addison Mizner's unique South Florida look. You can find a home here for less than $300,000.

Neighbors: Depending on where you live in this city, your neighbors could be city-dwelling retirees, business and finance professionals, young couples, families, blue-collar workers or twenty-something singles. The average age of a West Palm Beach resident is 32 years old with a median income of $60,492. West Palm Beach tends to have a higher percentage of singles than places like Jupiter or Palm Beach Gardens.

Source: Discover the Palm Beaches
Clematis Street nightlife draws young professionals to West Palm Beach's downtown.

School Report Card: AreaVibes gives West Palm Beach schools a score of "C+". GreatSchools gives the community schools an overall score of 5 out of 10.

Names to Know: Clematis Street, CityPlace, Antique Row, Okeechobee Boulevard, Palm Beach Atlantic University, The Palm Beach Post, and Mayor Jeri Muoio.

Wellington

Located just 12 miles west of West Palm Beach, the Village of Wellington is truly the equestrian capital of America. The town contains miles upon miles of equestrian trails, beautiful pastures, horse communities, and posh polo clubs, including the famed International Polo Club Palm Beach. Palm Beach County residents flock to Wellington for the town's annual horse show, polo matches, and various social events throughout the year. In 2010, Wellington was included in *Money Magazine's* "Top 100 Best Places to Live" list. It's safe to say that Wellington is a fabulous choice for those who own horses and prefer quiet communities miles away from the city's bright lights.

What Your Money Can Buy: Wellington is often referred to as a "bedroom community" in Palm Beach County, which sprung from an abundance of inexpensive land. The rural area is made up of multiple Planned Urban Developments, or PUDS as they're called, which range in price and type of residents. Planned communities in Wellington exist for just about every type of owner, including: retirement communities for the 55-plus age group, single family homes for first time homeowners seeking less expensive real estate, and sprawling equestrian estates for the horse lovers. Rental availability is relatively low and prices are quite high. The average rental rate is around $2,000 a month. If you're looking to buy, the median listing price in Wellington is $315,000, however, many of Wellington's larger equestrian estates, like those in the exclusive Mallet Hill neighborhood, are priced in the millions.

Neighbors: The "village" contains roughly 60,000 people, 79 percent of whom are married. With an average age of 43 years old, Wellington residents include retirees and wealthy upper-class folks with horses, farms, and a general love for Polo, often called the "Sport of Kings."

School Report Card: AreaVibes gives Wellington schools a score of "A". GreatSchools gives the community schools a score of 8 out of 10.

Names to Know: The International Polo Club Palm Beach, "Vanilla
Ice," Tommy Lee Jones, Bruce Springsteen, Winter Equestrian
Festival, "Flying Cow Ranch," The Mall at Wellington Green, Michael
Bloomberg, and Nacho Figueras (model and Argentine polo player).

Lake Worth

Named after the body of water on its eastern border, Lake Worth is one
of the most unique and diverse towns in the area. The community is
home to 40,000 people within its six square miles and offers residents
a bustling arts scene. In fact, it is even home to the world's largest street
painting festival. Visitors will find Lake Worth residents celebrating
the weekend at local beach bonfires, sipping lattes at downtown coffee
houses, and perusing Saturday farmers markets. A mix of old and
new, Lake Worth also boasts a vast array of historic buildings in its
revitalized downtown.

What Your Money Can Buy: Like its neighbor to the south, Boynton
Beach, real estate in Lake Worth is quite affordable. The average
rent price for a one-bedroom unit is $918 per month, while two-
bedroom rentals will only cost you around $1,515. The median listing
price for a home in Lake Worth is around $225,000—you can find
single family homes in the $100,000 to $300,000 range fairly easily.
Housing options in this town mostly consist of townhomes, condos,
and single family homes.

Neighbors: Lake Worth is home to an eclectic bunch. You'll find
many of the residents to be in their 20's and 30's, and many that are
renters. Expect to meet artists, musicians, blue-collar workers, white-
collar professionals, singles, young couples, and immigrants.

School Report Card: AreaVibes gives Lake Worth schools a score of
"D+". GreatSchools gives the community schools a score of 6 out of
10.

Names to Know: Lake Worth Lagoon, General William J. Worth (led
troops during the Second Seminole War), Samuel and Fannie James
(Lake Worth's first settlers), the Barefoot Mailman (mail carriers on the
first U.S. mail route), and The William O. Lockhart Municipal Pier

Other Central County communities to consider include: Lantana, Hypoluxo, Royal Palm Beach, Greenacres, and Atlantis.

South County

Boynton Beach

With over 66,000 residents, Boynton Beach is the third largest city in Palm Beach County, behind West Palm and Boca Raton. Despite being a highly popular place to live, the city lacks an official downtown hub. However, this could all change in the coming decade because, like its neighboring towns, Boynton Beach is also in the midst of a revitalization. Lately, area residents and city officials have been pushing for the redevelopment of the Boynton Harbor Marina, which could result in a more centralized downtown area.

Source: Dana McMahon
Marina Village in Boynton Beach.

What Your Money Can Buy: Real estate in Boynton Beach is generally more affordable than in its close neighbors, Delray Beach and Boca Raton. For instance, a one-story house in Boynton could cost anywhere from $275,000 to $350,000, while a one-story house in Delray Beach that is east of Interstate-95 will cost an average of $325,000 to $450,000. Real estate in Boynton Beach consists of condos, apartments, townhouses, and single-family homes. Single family home construction and many of the 55-plus communities in Boynton Beach have both continued to push west into neighborhoods, such as the ones located adjacent to Lyons Road. For reference, the section of Lyons Road connecting Boynton Beach Boulevard and West Atlantic Avenue opened back in 2013, allowing residents to traverse between the towns more easily while avoiding the often congested Florida Turnpike and Jog Road. Valencia Reserve and Canyon Lakes communities are both great options in the west Boynton Beach area.

For those looking to rent, the average rental rate for a two-bedroom unit in Boynton Beach will cost about $1,700. The popular Marina Village high-rises, located on the Intracoastal Waterway, offer condos for rent and for sale. Condos with water views in this building are fairly affordable, coming in under half-a-million. Marina Village rentals are priced in the $3,000 a month range.

Neighbors: You can expect to meet plenty of Baby Boomer retirees in the 60 to 65 age range. Boynton Beach is also an economical option for young couples buying their first homes, middle class families, and young professionals looking for an affordable condo near the water with easy access to their boat.

School Report Card: AreaVibes gives Boynton Beach schools a score of "B". GreatSchools gives the community schools a score of 6 out of 10.

Names to Know: Nathan Boynton (Boynton Beach's namesake), Vince Wilfork (NFL player), and Boynton Beach Boulevard.

Delray Beach

Named "Most Fun Small Town in America" by Rand McNally and USA Today, Delray Beach is filled with dozens of first-class restaurants, cafes, art galleries, boutiques, and white sandy beaches. Atlantic Avenue (or "the Ave." as the locals call it) is constantly buzzing with outdoor concerts, festivals, and events. Delray Beach has an official population of more than 60,000 people, but many of its snowbird and "snowflake" residents don't fly down until the high season.

What Your Money Can Buy: Delray Beach offers townhouses, loft style apartments, and of course, condos and oceanfront homes. Delray Beach also has a selection of older, single family homes and gated communities in historic areas like Lake Ida, where houses cost between $400,000 to $2 million. The median listing price for homes in Delray Beach is $280,000, however, prices are higher in the more desirable areas east of Swinton Avenue, and they're only increasing. Rule of thumb: the closer the home is to the waterfront, the more expensive it will be. Generally, Delray Beach's waterfront homes in neighborhoods like Palm Trail, the Marina Historic District, and Tropic Isles can cost millions.

Source: Dana McMahon
Condos and boutiques line Delray's Pineapple Grove District.

As for renting, the average rental rate for a two-bedroom unit in Delray Beach hovers around $2,500. If you're looking to live near Atlantic Avenue, I suggest looking at places like: the Pineapple Grove Arts District with two-bedroom rental units ranging from $2,000 to $3,000 a month; the newly opened SOFA complex; or Worthing Place, a luxury apartment building located in the heart of Delray Beach. Other popular complexes near Atlantic Avenue that offer condos for sale and for rent include: Mallory Square, The Astor, Latitude Delray, and Ocean City Lofts. Secure complexes like Alta Congress and Villas d'Este are other good rental options for those looking to live west of I-95.

Neighbors: Delray Beach is a diverse community, filled with both retirees and young professionals looking for a walkable, pet-friendly small town environment with fabulous restaurants and a stunning beach. You'll meet everyone from wealthy snowbirds and young couples to singles and retirees.

School Report Card: AreaVibes gives Delray Beach schools a score of "B". GreatSchools gives the community schools a score of 6 out of 10.

Names to Know: Kevin James (actor), Pineapple Grove, and William S. Linton (founder).

Boca Raton

With a population of 91,000 people in its 30 square miles, Boca Raton is massive compared to surrounding towns. Coming in as the second largest city in the Palm Beaches, this sprawling metropolis marks the southern tip of Palm Beach County, and is often referred to as "the Beverly Hills of South Florida." In 2014, CreditDonkey named Boca the number one place to live in Florida because of its low crime rate, above average incomes, and short commute times.

Once thought of as an exclusive destination for wealthy New Yorkers (thanks in large part to *Seinfeld*), Boca Raton has now become accessible to all, as more and more housing communities push west. However, it is still home to several of the most expensive gated communities in the country.

On any given day, you can catch Boca Ratonians strolling down the gorgeous beaches, eating at one of the city's tasty restaurants or enjoying an outdoor concert at Mizner Park's amphitheater. Boca is also well-known in Palm Beach for its fabulous shopping. Experience retail therapy galore at Boca's outdoor shopping and dining center, Mizner Park or at Town Center. Boca Raton also happens to be home to a thriving tech industry as well as the global headquarters of Office Depot.

Source: Discover the Palm Beaches
One of the many mega mansions along the Intracoastal Waterway.

What Your Money Can Buy: Generally, people divide the city into East Boca (Boca Raton) and West Boca (also called Boca West). The latter is an unincorporated community west of the Florida's Turnpike. Boca West is considered less crowded than the eastern part of Boca Raton, and has mostly new home construction with a median listing price at $139,000. Farther east in Boca Raton's coastal communities, the average single family home price rises significantly in cost. The median listing price for a home here is generally around $389,000. Despite the low crime rate, Boca Raton has a high number of gated communities—as well as numerous golf course communities and country clubs. Waterfront homes are especially expensive—many cost over $10 million. I recommend taking a sightseeing cruise down the Intracoastal Waterway past East Boca's many breathtakingly grand estates.

Besides single family homes, there are also plenty of apartments and condos for newcomers in both East Boca and Boca West. The average price of a two-bedroom rental unit is relatively expensive, costing around $2,520.

Source: Dana McMahon
Mizner Park Apartments in downtown Boca Raton

Neighbors: With a median age of 45 years old and many of its residents in the 50-plus age bracket, Boca Raton is home to an older crowd—many of whom have relocated from up north. However, there is also a handful of young professionals. A mix of white-collar businessmen and tech entrepreneurs, retirees, snowbirds, DINKS ("Dual Income No Kids" couples), and upper to middle class families make up the majority of this large city.

School Report Card: AreaVibes gives Boca Raton schools a score of "A". GreatSchools gives the community schools a score of 9 out of 10.

Names to Know: Addison Mizner, Boca Raton Resort & Club, Florida Atlantic University, Glades Road, Ariana Grande (singer), Sheryl Sandberg, Jozy Altidore (soccer player), Adam Sandler, and Jon Bon Jovi.

Other South County communities to consider: Highland Beach, Gulf Stream, Briny Breezes, Ocean Ridge, and Manalapan.

*Source: All home listing price estimates in this chapter are based on data from Realtor.com, as well as information gathered from various realtors in Palm Beach County.

CHAPTER NINE
CAN YOU LIVE WELL HERE?

"The Sunshine State attracts folks from across the globe... As the fourth largest economy in the U.S., the second largest job creator after California... Florida has also cultivated a reputation as one of the best states in which to raise kids." —WalletHub

Source: Christopher Fay Photography
Palm Beach County offers a fantastic lifestyle for families.

Why do so many people purchase a one-way ticket to the Palm Beaches and never look back? It's because, despite being the wealthiest county in the state, newcomers can actually afford to live here. Plus, the county's gorgeous coastline, great schools, and countless outdoor activities make living in the Palm Beaches a no-brainer for many. Here's a look at the county's overall cost of living and resident services.

Overall Cost of Living

According to City-Data.com, the overall cost of living in Palm Beach County is roughly on par with the the national average. Of course, each Palm Beach County town's housing prices, services, and overall cost of living varies. In the chart below, you can compare various Palm Beach County towns' overall cost of living—from highest to lowest—compared to the national cost of living. *Note: The higher the Index, the higher the cost of living.*

Location	Cost of Living Index
National	100
Florida	101
Palm Beach	183
Highland Beach	163
Boca Raton	128
Juno Beach	125
Wellington	121
Jupiter	120
Tequesta	120
Palm Beach Gardens	119
North Palm Beach	111
Delray Beach	108
West Palm Beach	105
Boynton Beach	101
Riviera Beach/ Singer Island	100
Lantana	99
Lake Worth	97
Belle Glade	91

Source: AreaVibes

According to Numbeo, West Palm Beach's cost of living is well below that of other mid-to-large East Coast cities. West Palm's home rental rates are nearly 43% lower than rental rates in Boston. Overall restaurant prices are also 4.6% lower than those found on the menus in Charleston, SC. Consumer prices including rent are 4.7% lower than those in our neighboring city of Miami, and grocery prices are about 5% lower than grocery prices in Washington, DC.

Housing

Real estate options in Palm Beach County are as varied as the population that lives here. Although the Palm Beaches has some of the most expensive estates in the country, it's also home to plenty of affordable residential areas. In fact, the cost of housing in places like Boynton Beach and Lake Worth are well below the national average.

Source: Carl Dawson of LivingExposure and the Delray Beach Downtown Development Authority
A lower cost of living means more shopping for this Delray Beach resident.

As of March 2016, the average listing price in Palm Beach County was $300,000, while the average closing price came in at $210,000, according to <u>Realtor.com</u>. Palm Beach County's largest city, West Palm Beach, had a median listing price of $225,000 and a median closing price of $150,000. The average per-square-foot home price in West Palm Beach was $156. When compared to other cities, like Miami ($268), Boston ($437), Washington, DC ($407), and Austin ($179), West Palm's housing prices start to sound pretty reasonable.

More home price examples in the area: Home buyers can find a two-bedroom, two-bathroom single-family home, west of Interstate-95 in Boynton Beach, for around $170,000. A two-bedroom, two-bathroom condominium in downtown West Palm Beach can be found for roughly $289,000 at the popular Prado building. A three-bedroom, three-bathroom townhouse in Jupiter's desirable Abacoa area can be found for around $350,000.

Compare these prices to the median sales prices in other desirable parts of the country:

- $350,000: North Buckhead area of Atlanta, Georgia

- $628,800: Northeast Coconut Grove neighborhood of Miami, Florida

- $400,000: Lincoln Park neighborhood of Chicago, Illinois

- $1,420,000: Park Slope neighborhood of Brooklyn, New York

- $201,000: West Ashley neighborhood of Charleston, SC

- $405,000: South End neighborhood of Boston, Massachusetts

- $1,720,000: Noe Valley neighborhood of San Francisco, California

- $431,200: Logan Circle neighborhood of Washington, DC

Source: Trulia.com

As you might expect, waterfront homes on both the Intracoastal Waterway and the Atlantic Ocean are pricier. In general, the farther east the real estate, the more expensive it will be—as is the case in Delray Beach, Boca Raton, and West Palm Beach. In many towns like Palm Beach Gardens and Jupiter, you should also prepare yourself for hefty equity membership fees that often come with the perks of moving to a golf course or country club residential community.

Utilities

Electricity

The majority of Palm Beach County residents receive their power from **Florida Power and Light** (FPL). The company is the third largest electric utility in the U.S. and happens to be located right here in Juno Beach. While living in Palm Beach County isn't always cheap, you'll be happy to hear that residents save a pretty penny when it comes to their electric bills. The typical 1,000-kWh residential customer bill with FPL is 30% lower than the national average. It's also the lowest in Florida and among the lowest in the nation when it comes to utility bills. In even better news—Florida Power and Light rates have decreased even further in 2016. Residents have seen their bills go down by $2.50 a month on average.

To estimate your monthly savings, FPL provides an online bill calculator on its website at www.fpl.com.

I should note, however, that many Lake Worth residents do not use Florida Power and Light. Instead, they rely on their own local utilities company, Lake Worth Utilities. These bills are, on average, slightly higher than FPL's monthly bills. According to the *Palm Beach Post*, a typical 1,000-kWh residential customer bill in 2014 for FPL was $107.84. While a bill for Lake Worth Utilities costs customers $115.53.

Water-Sewer

The Palm Beach County Water Utilities Department provides drinking water for residents throughout the Palm Beaches. Our drinking water is drawn from wells, which tap into a large underground aquifer. The utility produces over 100 million gallons per day of drinking water for Palm Beach residents. According to www.pbcgov.com, the typical usage for a single-family home is around 250 gallons per day. The average monthly water bill in Florida is $58.37 for a single-family home.

Source: Palm Beach County Water Utilities Department's Annual Water Quality Report

Taxes

It's no secret that Florida's state income taxes—or lack thereof—happen to be one of the Sunshine State's major selling points for potential newcomers. In fact, according to the Tax Foundation, the State of Florida has the fourth-best business tax climate in the nation.

Our state does not tax individual income, intangible personal property, inheritance or gifts. Floridians are also not required to shell out a vehicle property tax, either. However, residents are required to pay several taxes and fees, depending on where they live and what they do. In Palm Beach County, local businesses, including home-based companies, are required to pay the Local Business Tax. A Tourist Development Tax is issued to owners of a unit that has been rented or leased for six months or less.

Tax-Savings Scenarios

$1 Million Income/Personal State & City Income Tax

FLORIDA	NEW YORK	CONNECTICUT
$0	$104,300	$67,000

Estate Tax on $25 Million

FLORIDA	NEW YORK	CONNECTICUT
$0	$3,466,800	$2,536,200

Gain from Business/Property Sale of $100 Million

FLORIDA	NEW YORK	CONNECTICUT
$0	$12,692,774	$6,700,000

Tax Rate Comparison

	FLORIDA	NEW YORK	CONNECTICUT
Top marginal individual tax rate	0%	12.70%	6.70%
Top marginal estate tax rate	0%	16.00%	12.00%
Top marginal capital gains tax rate	0%	12.70%	6.70%
Corporate tax rate	5.50%	8.87%	7.50%
Unincorporated tax rate	0%	4.00%	0%
Highest sales tax rate	6.00%	9.00%	6.35%

Source: Chart courtesy of the Business Development Board of Palm Beach County

Here in Florida, our Property Taxes aren't particularly high compared to other states, but they also aren't particularly low either. According to WalletHub, Florida is the 29th best state in terms of property taxes. The average Florida resident pays $1,913 each year in property taxes for their homes, compared to the national average of $2,089. The property tax rate varies by community, with the island of Palm Beach's rate notably higher than other towns. Permanent Florida residents also benefit significantly by qualifying for a Florida Homestead Exemption. This important money-saving exemption entitles homeowners in the State of Florida to a sizable deduction off of their home's assessed property value. This means that homeowners in Florida may be able to save quite a bundle on their property taxes.

According to www.pbcgov.com:

Homestead Exemption is granted to permanent Florida residents only. The property must be your permanent residence. A permanent residence is the address listed on your voter's registration card, driver's license or ID, the place where you register your cars and file your income tax. If you or your spouse are receiving a residence based exemption or benefit in another county, state or country, you are not eligible for exemption.

Healthcare

From award-winning hospitals and top-notch doctors to world-renowned treatment centers and a plethora of clinic options, Palm Beach County is home to stellar healthcare services. Here's a look at some of the best places in the county for fulfilling your quality healthcare needs.

Hospitals and Clinics

When it comes to hospitals, Palm Beach County has numerous quality options. Recently, seven area hospitals were even ranked among the best in the country by the The Joint Commission, a U.S. healthcare inspection and accreditation organization. These top performing hospitals included:

JFK Medical Center – www.jfkmc.com – Located in Atlantis, JFK Medical Center is a 472-bed acute care medical and surgical facility known for its 24-hour emergency services, cardiovascular care, cancer care, breast care, neurosciences, stroke care, and orthopedic care—among others.

Delray Medical Center – www.delraymedicalctr.com – This Delray Beach facility is a 493-bed acute care hospital that serves as both a community hospital and a Level I Trauma Center. The hospital's specialized services include cardiac care, orthopedics, and rehabilitation—among others.

Palm Beach Gardens Medical Center – www.pbgmc.com – Palm Beach Gardens Medical Center is a 199-bed acute care hospital offering a wide range of treatments, from heart care to advanced brain and neurological services.

Palms West Hospital in Loxahatchee – www.palmswesthospital.com – Located in Loxahatchee, this 204-bed facility offers top-quality care with a full-service emergency care facility specializing in pediatrics, orthopedics and cardiac care.

West Palm Hospital – www.westpalmhospital.com – This 245-bed acute care facility, located in West Palm Beach, includes an adjoining

88-bed psychiatric unit and a medical professional office building housing West Palm Hospital's specialty outpatient rehabilitation center, a comprehensive breast center, and more.

Good Samaritan Medical Center – www.goodsamaritanmc.com – Located in West Palm Beach, this award-winning 333-bed acute care hospital offers a broad range of services including internal medicine, general surgery, cardiology, orthopedics, oncology, delivery, and surgical weight loss.

In 2015, it was announced that West Palm Hospital was merging with JFK Medical Center to become JFK Medical Center North Campus. According to the *South Florida Business Journal*, it is the largest medical center in Palm Beach County with more than 2,600 employees and 717 beds.

Other hospitals and clinics worth noting:

Boca Raton Regional Hospital – www.brrh.com – *U.S. News and World Report recently* ranked the Boca Raton Regional Hospital the 12th best hospital in Florida. The not-for-profit, advanced tertiary medical center provides 400 beds and more than 800 primary and specialty physicians on staff.

Jupiter Medical Center – www.jupitermed.com – This hospital is a not-for-profit, 327-bed regional medical center located in Jupiter, FL. This hospital was also the recipient of the ATHENA Award in Business by the Chamber of Commerce of the Palm Beaches.

Nicklaus Children's Hospital – www.nicklauschildrens.org – This hospital provides several outpatient centers throughout South Florida, one of which is the Palm Beach Outpatient Center in Palm Beach Gardens.

St. Mary's Medical Center – www.stmarysmc.com – A 464-bed hospital, which includes the Palm Beach Children's Hospital. It is located in West Palm Beach.

West Palm VA Medical Center – www.westpalmbeach.va.gov – A general medical, psychiatric, and surgical facility in West Palm Beach.

It provides a wide range of services to veterans, as well as several outpatient centers throughout the county.

Cleveland Clinic Florida – www.my.clevelandclinic.org – The not-for-profit hospital integrates clinical and hospital care with research. The hospital ranked ninth in Florida in *US News & World Report's* 2015-2016 ranking of Best Hospitals metro area rankings.

C.L. Brumback Primary Care Clinic – www.clbrumbackprimary careclinics.org – The clinic offers adult and pediatric medical care throughout its multiple locations in Palm Beach County.

Addiction Treatment Centers

According to *Florida Trend*, Palm Beach County has the highest concentration of "high-end" addiction treatment centers in the eastern United States. For a more detailed look at various rehab centers in the county, you can check out the www.PsychologyToday.com list of local treatment centers.

How Safe Is Palm Beach County?

Generally speaking, areas with more tourists tend to have more crime, particularly in the city centers and downtowns. West Palm Beach is no exception. Patches of this city—just like any other big city—can be dicey. The good news is non-violent crime has fortunately been on the decline as of late. West Palm Beach, in particular, has made great strides in decreasing crime with heavy and visible police patrol in the downtown area.

In 2015, the *Sun Sentinel* reported that Palm Beach County saw a 5.2% decrease in its crime rate. Towns like Delray Beach, Boynton Beach, and West Palm Beach experienced a noticeable drop in crime, according to the Florida Department of Law Enforcement.

Several Palm Beach County cities also landed in the top 60 on ValuePenguin's 2015 "Safest Cities in Florida" list. These towns included: Highland Beach, Palm Beach, North Palm Beach, Jupiter, Boca Raton, Wellington, Palm Beach Gardens, and Juno Beach. You can see the full list on www.valuepenguin.com.

CHAPTER TEN
THE ECONOMIC CLIMATE

"Palm Beach County's economy is going through a transformation—from an economy that was built on construction, tourism, and real estate to one that is now centered around technology and innovation."

—Kelly Smallridge, President of the Business Development Board of Palm Beach County

Our thriving job market, skilled workforce, and superior tax benefits are just several of the major incentives for moving to Palm Beach County. Here's a look at our booming economic climate.

Source: Discover the Palm Beaches
West Palm Beach's financial hub

A Snapshot of Our Top Industries

Agriculture

A whopping 456,001 acres of county land are used for agricultural purposes, making it one of the top ten county leaders in agriculture in the U.S. Palm Beach County also led the State of Florida in agricultural sales for 2014-15 with an estimated $1.38 billion. Our county leads the nation in the production of sugarcane, fresh sweet corn, and sweet bell peppers.

Aviation, Aerospace, and Engineering

Palm Beach County has over 20,000 employees working in this innovative industry. Major employers include Sikorsky Aircraft Corporation (a manufacturer of Black Hawk helicopters), Lockheed Martin, Pratt Whitney, Aerojet Rocketdyne, and B/E Aerospace, a leading manufacturer of jet aircraft passenger-cabin interior products.

Business and Financial Services

When it comes to jobs, the business and financial services industry accounts for roughly 24% of them in Palm Beach County—and that number is only rising. In 2014, Mayor Jeri Muoio designated an area in West Palm Beach as the "Flagler Financial District," in an effort to reposition the city as a major financial hub for investment-oriented companies on the East Coast. So far, 300 hedge funds and private equity firms from all over the world have opened offices in South Florida, thanks to the area's tax-saving benefits, easy access to Latin and Caribbean markets, multilingual workforce, and first-rate South Florida lifestyle.

Construction

As you're sure to notice, there is a staggering amount of construction and development happening here in Palm Beach County. Given the growing number of businesses and the increasing population, construction provides a significant boost to local employment.

Equestrian

Not only is our Palm Beach International Equestrian Center the most well-known equestrian venue in the country, but our Winter Equestrian Festival (WEF) is the largest and longest-running circuit in equestrian sports. During the polo season, it's estimated that over 250,000 people attend the show over the 12-week circuit that runs from January to April.

Healthcare

Our state-of-the-art hospitals and 4,800 healthcare-related businesses make our healthcare system a major sector of the Palm Beach County economy. The industry accounts for 80,000 jobs and has been recognized nation-wide for its top performing hospitals, according to the The Joint Commission.

IT and Telecommunications

In the 1980's, IBM's invention of the PC in Boca Raton launched our county's technology sector into the public eye. Since that time, Palm Beach County has continued to attract leading software developers and telecommunication companies to its cities every year. The industry in Palm Beach County is only strengthened by our capable workforce and fantastic telecom infrastructure.

Life Sciences

South Florida is home to more than 1,200 life science companies, all of which provide a steady stream of biotech, pharmaceutical, manufacturing, and medical device jobs. Thanks to local life science research facilities like the Max Planck Florida Institute, Scripps Florida, and Florida Atlantic University, Palm Beach County is a powerhouse hub for the biotech industry.

Marine Industry

According to the Business Development Board, the marine industry has an annual direct economic impact of $1.35 billion. Our Palm Beach International Boat Show is one of the top ten boat shows in the U.S., with over $350 million worth of boats and yachts on display. The marine services industry in our county employs roughly 20,000 workers.

Tourism

The thriving tourism industry in the Palm Beaches is a key source of revenue and business for the county. Every year, over 2 million people visit and vacation in our area, bringing in billions of dollars worth of revenue. The tourism industry in the Palm Beaches creates over 53,000 service sector jobs throughout the county in hotels, restaurants, and retail.

Source: Facts and figures courtesy of the Business Development Board of Palm Beach County.

Top Employers

Palm Beach County's largest employer is the Palm Beach County School District, with around 22,000 employees in its 187 public schools. Take a look at Palm Beach County's top employers in the charts below.

Top Employers

Palm Beach County boasts some of the finest manufacturers in the world. Their presence is a strong indication of the county's ability to support the industry. Although the county has a variety of producers, there are distinct industry clusters. The most prevalent are: communications & information technology; aerospace & engineering; agriculture & food processing; business & financial services and life sciences, including medical & pharmaceutical products. Many of the county's industrial employers are competing on a worldwide basis with products sold in the international market. Below is a list of some of the largest quality companies that have chosen Palm Beach County as a business location.

Goods Producing

Company	Approx. Employees	Product	Location
Florida Crystals (Hdqtrs)	1,700*	Agriculture	West Palm Beach
Sikorsky Aircraft	1,181	Helicopters	West Palm Beach
U.S. Sugar Corp.	900	Agriculture	Belle Glade
Tyco (Hdqrts)	850*	Security System Manufacturing	Boca Raton/West Palm Beach
TBC Corporation (Hdqtrs)	807	Tire Distribution	Palm Beach Gardens
Walgreens Distribution	715*	Pharmaceutical Distribution	Jupiter
Pratt & Whitney *(A United Technologies Company)*	675	Jet Engine Manufacturing	West Palm Beach
Cheney Brothers	660	Food Distribution	Riviera Beach
ADT Security Services (Hdqtrs)	600	Security System Manufacturing	Boca Raton/West Palm Beach
IBM Corp.	600*	Electronics R&D	Boca Raton
PSM, An Alstom Company	500	Turbine Parts Manufacturing	Jupiter
US Foods	500	Food Distribution	Boca Raton
BIOMET 3i, Inc.	471	Dental Implants	Palm Beach Gardens
Belcan Engineering Group	420	Aerospace Engineering	Palm Beach Gardens
Lockheed Martin Corporation	406	Aerospace Engineering	Riviera Beach
Aerojet Rocketdyne *(A GenCorp Company)*	400	Aerospace Engineering	West Palm Beach

*Updated figures unavailable at date of publication
Sources: Updates provided by the employers Year Ending 2014

Top Employers

Service companies, both public and private, large and small, support the area's residents and businesses. There are roughly 52,315 companies in Palm Beach County that supply products and services. In the services producing sector of the economy, a strong cluster of companies is found in business and financial services. This cluster represents more than 19,158 companies. Below is a list of just a few of the major service oriented employers in Palm Beach County.

Company	Approx. Employees	Product	Location
Palm Beach County School District	22,000	Education	County Wide
Tenet Healthcare Corp.	6,100	Healthcare	County Wide
Palm Beach County *(Board of Commissioners)*	5,507	County Government	West Palm Beach
NextEra Energy, Inc. (Hdqtrs) *(The parent company of Florida Power & Light)*	3,854	Utilities	Juno Beach
HCA Palm Beach Hospitals *(JFK, Palms West and West Palm)*	2,714*	Healthcare	County Wide
Florida Atlantic University	2,655	Higher Education	Boca Raton
Bethesda Memorial Hospital	2,600	Health Care	Boynton Beach
Boca Raton Regional Hospital	2,500	Health Care	Boca Raton
Veterans Health Administration	2,500	Health Care	West Palm Beach
Jupiter Medical Center	2,000	Health Care	Jupiter
Office Depot (Hdqtrs)	2,000*	Office Supplies	Boca Raton
The Breakers	2,000	Hotel	Palm Beach
Wells Fargo	1,367	Financial Services	County Wide
City of West Palm Beach	1,326	City Government	West Palm Beach
Boca Raton Resort & Club	1,292*	Hotel	Boca Raton
City of Boca Raton	1,228	City Government	Boca Raton
Palm Beach State College	1,155	Higher Education	Lake Worth
G4S Secure Solutions, USA (Hdqtrs)	1,100	Security Services	Palm Beach Gardens

*Updated figures unavailable at date of publication
Sources: Updates provided by the employers Year Ending 2014

*Source: Charts courtesy of the Business Development Board of Palm Beach County

Information on Relocating Your Business or Employees to Palm Beach County

Why the Palm Beaches Is the Perfect Place to Relocate Your Company and Employees

by Kelly Smallridge, President & CEO of the Business Development Board of Palm Beach County

Palm Beach County is one of the hottest business markets in the State of Florida. With 40 miles of pristine beaches, a diversified workforce, access to three airports, the Port of Palm Beach, the arts, recreational opportunities, affordable commercial and residential real estate along with quality public and private schools, this area is booming with companies of all sizes.

Companies relocating to Palm Beach County are in the areas of aerospace, financial services, corporate headquarters, life sciences, manufacturing, logistics and distribution, and technology. There is a strong entrepreneurial spirit that has led to the area also being recognized as a top destination for entrepreneurs. To receive more information on relocating a company to Palm Beach County, confidential and complimentary services are provided by the Business Development Board of Palm Beach County. Please contact Brian Cartland at 561-835-1008 or visit www.bdb.org.

CHAPTER ELEVEN

QUALITY EDUCATION IN THE PALM BEACHES

Our school district, with its 185 schools and 183,000 students, is the 11th largest in the nation and the fifth largest in Florida. To get a truly in-depth look at our county's school offerings—from private and faith-based K-12 to public K-12 and universities—I highly recommend visiting the Business Development Board's "Education Information" website at www.pbcedu.org.

Public Schools

With so many choices, finding the right school for your child can seem overwhelming. In Palm Beach County, students can attend a local school they are zoned for or they can attend one of the many Choice Program schools. These schools have a specialization in everything from the culinary arts and STEM to Montessori and theater. The majority of schools with Choice Programs accept students through a lottery method. To look at the list of programs offered by each school, you can visit **The School District of Palm Beach County website** at www.palmbeachschools.org/choiceprograms/high.asp.

Charter Schools are another public school option for parents in the Palm Beaches. As of 2015, the Palm Beach County School District was the sponsor of 50 charter schools throughout the county. Charter Schools are public schools that offer an alternative education to the traditional public school curriculum.

Source: Discover the Palm Beaches
The South Florida Science Center and Aquarium offers exciting
interactive science exhibits, engaging camps, and events for kids and families.

Quick facts from the Business Development Board of Palm Beach County:

- "The 10,000 Palm Beach County public school graduates in 2012 garnered nearly $94 million dollars in scholarships."

- "Over 92% of our high school graduates pursue college and other post-graduate education."

- "Education Week recognized the School District of Palm Beach County as having the second-highest graduation rates in the state, exceeding the state average, and the eighth-best in the nation. *Newsweek* and *U.S. News Magazine* ranked two of our public high schools in the Top 10 in the state, and *The Washington Post* ranked those same two in the Top 100 in the nation (2013)."

Source: www.pbcedu.org

Public School Ratings

Palm Beach County's public schools stand out, not just in Florida, but across the country. Recently, two of our public schools were even included in *U.S. News & World Report's* 2015 Best High Schools in America list:

The Alexander W. Dreyfoos School of the Arts – www.awdsoa.org – Located near CityPlace in West Palm Beach, the A.W. Dreyfoos School of the Arts provides students with an art-centered education in addition to an excellent academic program. The school attracts students with exceptional abilities in communication arts, dance, music, theatre, digital media or visual arts.

Suncoast High – www.edline.net/pages/Suncoast_High_School – Located in Riviera Beach, Suncoast High School is a public magnet high school with selective admissions. The school offers four magnet programs: Math, Science, and Engineering; Computer Science; International Baccalaureate (IB); or Innovative Interactive Technology Program.

Below is a chart of the top ranked public schools in several of the most popular Palm Beach County towns. The chart shows public schools with a GreatSchools rating of 8 or higher, based on the organization's 1 through 10 scale. A GreatSchools rating of 8-10 indicates that the school is ranked "above average."

Jupiter	GreatSchools Rating
Jupiter High School	9
Jupiter Middle School	9
Jupiter Farms Elementary School	10
Jerry Thomas Elementary School	8
Limestone Creek Elementary School	9
Beacon Cove Intermediate School	10
Independence Middle School	9

Palm Beach Gardens	GreatSchools Rating
Allamanda Elementary School	8
Watson B. Duncan Middle School	9
Timber Trace Elementary School	10
Marsh Pointe Elementary School	10

Wellington	GreatSchools Rating
Wellington High School	8
Wellington Landings Middle School	10
Palm Beach Central High School	8
Equestrian Trails Elementary School	10
Binks Forest Elementary School	10
Polo Park Middle School	10
Elbridge Gale Elementary School	8
Emerald Cove Middle School	8

Palm Beach	GreatSchools Rating
Palm Beach Public School	8

West Palm Beach	GreatSchools Rating
Alexander W. Dreyfoos Junior School of the Arts	10
BAK Middle School of the Arts	10
South Olive Elementary School	9
Western Pines Community Middle School	9
Palm Beach Virtual Franchise	9
Pine Jog Elementary School	9
Everglades Elementary School	9
G-Star School of the Arts	8

Meadow Park Elementary School	8
Cypress Trails Elementary School	8
Golden Grove Elementary School	8
Palm Beach Virtual Instruction Program	8

Lake Worth	GreatSchools Rating
Panther Run Elementary School	9
Manatee Elementary School	10
Coral Reef Elementary School	9
Discovery Key Elementary School	9
Park Vista Community High School	8
Academy for Positive Learning	8

Delray Beach	GreatSchools Rating
Morikami Park Elementary School	10
S.D. Spady Elementary School	8
Banyan Creek Elementary School	8

Boynton Beach	GreatSchools Rating
Ben Gamla-Palm Beach	10
Sunset Palm Elementary School	10
Somerset Academy Canyons High School	9
Christa Mcauliffe Middle School	8
Freedom Shores Elementary School	8
Crosspointe Elementary School	8

Boca Raton	GreatSchools Rating
Boca Raton Community High School	10

Addison Mizner Elementary School	10
Del Prado Elementary School	10
Water's Edge Elementary School	10
A.D. Henderson University School & Fau High School	10
Don Estridge High Tech Middle School	10
J.C. Mitchell Elementary School	9
Spanish River Community High School	9
Verde Elementary School	9
Calusa Elementary School	9
Sandpiper Shores Elementary School	9
Omni Middle School	9
Eagles Landing Middle School	9
Sunrise Park Elementary School	9
West Boca Raton High School	9
Somerset Academy Boca Middle School	9
Boca Raton Community High School	8
Whispering Pines Elementary School	8
Coral Sunset Elementary School	8

Private Schools

According to Private School Review, there are over 26,000 students enrolled in Palm Beach County private schools. Recently, two of our county's private schools landed in the top 25 list of Niche.com's Florida private schools rankings. The list included the top 100 private schools in Florida, based on student statistics and opinions from both students and parents. The local schools that made the list were:

- **The Benjamin School**, located in North Palm Beach and Palm Beach Gardens.

- **Saint Andrew's School** in Boca Raton.

For a look at the rankings, you can visit www.k12.niche.com/rankings/ private-high-schools/best-overall/s/florida

The Benjamin School – www.thebenjaminschool.org – The Benjamin School is a pre-k through 12, college prep day school in Palm Beach County. The private school boasts a 100% college acceptance rate, a strong athletic program, and the lowest student:teacher ratio in the State of Florida for a pre-k through grade 12 school. The rigorous academic program includes 15 years of language instruction, as well as plenty of Advanced Placement class offerings. The school is just as well-known for its academic rigor as it is for the students who walk the halls. Celebrities like golfer Tiger Woods and singer Celine Dion have sent their children to The Benjamin School over the years. Golf icon Jack Nicklaus' grandchildren have attended as well.

Source: Discover the Palm Beaches
The Loggerhead Marine Lifecenter in Juno Beach hosts field trips, outreach programs, summer camp, and other educational programs for thousands of school children every year.

Saint Andrew's School – www.saintandrews.net – Unlike The Benjamin School, Saint Andrew's in Boca Raton is both a day and boarding college prep school. The pre-k through grade 12 private institution serves more than 1,200 students from all over the world and offers an International Baccalaureate (IB) World School. It's been deemed a "Green School of Excellence" due to its excellent facilities and offers everything from a rock climbing wall and dance studio to a newly renovated track and field facility.

For a full list of the excellent private schools in Palm Beach County, check out Private School Review's website at www.privateschoolreview. com/florida/palm-beach-county.

Evaluating Your Education Choices

Education in Palm Beach County—It's All About Choices

by Vicki Pugh

Palm Beach County families have an array of choices when it comes to education. Boasting the 11th largest school district in the nation, Palm Beach County's "A" rated public school system is the top urban school district in the State of Florida. One of its most popular offerings is the "Choice Program," which allows students seeking exposure to and experience in a specific field the opportunity for early career exploration.

The school district supports more than 250 Choice Programs and career academies beginning at the elementary school level. Students interested in careers in the sciences, education, music, entrepreneurship, law, technology, engineering, medical, business, languages, culinary, digital and visual arts, construction, dance, and many more, can apply for a choice program or career academy and receive hands-on experiences in their interest areas.

Charter schools are on the rise with 12,000+ students enrolled; students in grades K-12 have the option of taking classes online through Palm Beach Virtual and home education is supported through the school district and various homeschool networks throughout the county. There are close to 150 private schools in Palm Beach County, all offering intriguing alternatives to public education.

Local colleges and universities are forming stronger partnerships with schools, promoting STEAM (Science, Technology, Engineering, Art, and Math) initiatives and dual enrollment with new attempts to better prepare students for college and career. These partnerships include support from businesses and organizations that hope to grow a workforce for their own communities.

Four institutions of higher education have residential campuses in Palm Beach County, including Palm Beach Atlantic University, Florida Atlantic University, Palm Beach State College, and Keiser University. Branch campuses of Nova Southeastern, South, and other universities offer coursework for local, degree-seeking residents.

Palm Beach County offers something for every learner. This Mom is grateful to have so many choices!

Vicki Pugh serves as Vice President of Development for Palm Beach Atlantic University where she oversees fundraising and marketing initiatives. She is also the President of the Association of Fundraising Professionals Palm Beach County Chapter.

Higher Education

Palm Beach County has quite a few colleges and universities offering two-year and four-year degrees, as well as technical education centers and community schools with first-class vocational and occupational training.

Florida Atlantic University – www.fau.edu – FAU is a four-year college with campuses in both Boca Raton and Jupiter. The school offers undergraduate and graduate courses in everything from architecture and fine arts to business and engineering. The school is also home to the LifeLong Learning Society, one of the country's largest adult education institutions.

Palm Beach Atlantic University – www.pba.edu – Located in downtown West Palm Beach, Palm Beach Atlantic University is a Christian four-year university with a wide array of degrees, from biology to ministry.

Palm Beach State College – www.palmbeachstate.edu – This public state college serves nearly 50,000 students every year. It is the largest higher education institution in the county and offers over 100 academic programs at various campuses.

Lynn University – www.lynn.edu – Located in Boca Raton, the school is a private university noted for its diversity with over 2,500 students from all over the world.

Digital Media Arts College – www.dmac.edu – This Boca Raton-based school offers degrees in everything from computer animation and graphic design to web design and multimedia design.

Source: Palm Beach Atlantic University
The Palm Beach Atlantic University campus in West Palm Beach

Keiser University – www.keiseruniversity.edu – This school provides campuses and classes throughout Florida, including a West Palm Beach campus. The school offers small classes with programs focusing on criminal justice, nursing, and business—among others. Keiser University also offers working adults a flexible schedule with both online and evening classes.

Nova Southeastern University – www.nova.edu – Based in Fort Lauderdale, the university provides a Palm Beach Gardens campus to local students. Like Keiser University, this school also offers convenient scheduling for working adults. The school features day, evening, weekend, and online classes with degree programs in nursing, pharmacy, education, business, and respiratory therapy—among others.

Other local colleges and universities that offer convenient scheduling and online classes include **Everglades University** (www.evergladesuniversity.edu) and **South University** (www.southuniversity.edu/west-palm-beach).

Some of the best vocational, trade, and technical schools in Palm Beach County include **Career-Tech**, **Lincoln Tech**, **Empire Beauty School**, and **ITT Technical Institute**.

CHAPTER TWELVE
GETTING SETTLED

Moving to a new area of the country is never easy. Thankfully, in Palm Beach County the residents are as warm as the weather. One of the reasons for this is that many of the people living here are transplants themselves. Here's a quick overview of the best ways to network in this welcoming community.

Getting Involved in the Community

Meetup – www.meetup.com – This website provides a long list of various interest groups in your community. I strongly recommend joining to check out what is happening in your neighborhood. Whether it's a group of wine loving gal pals you're looking for or a group of like-minded professionals, you'll find them on Meetup. There are dance lesson meetups, 20 and 30-something mixer meetups, bike club meetups, outdoor adventure meetups, and of course, plenty of meetups for Palm Beach newbies.

Junior League – www.jlpb.org – Attention ladies: if you're interested in volunteering and meeting new friends, I suggest joining your local Junior League. Local chapters include the Junior League of the Palm Beaches and the Junior League of Boca Raton. I should note that another added benefit of joining the Junior League of the Palm Beaches is that members receive discounts at the PGA National Resort and Spa and the South Florida Science Center and Aquarium.

Young Friends of the Norton – www.norton.org/youngfriends – For those passionate about art, the Young Friends of the Norton Museum of Art is a great way to meet likeminded locals while taking advantage of our fabulous museum. The group enjoys access to educational and social events focusing on the museum's collections and exhibits. There are several different levels of membership. Suggested ages range from 21 to 49 years old.

Young Professionals of the Palm Beaches – www.palmbeaches.org/pages/ypop – If you're looking to meet young movers and shakers in the community, I suggest attending an event by the Young Professionals of the Palm Beaches. It is the largest and most active such organization in the county and provides great opportunities for networking.

Cultural Council of Palm Beach – www.palmbeachculture.com – The Cultural Council is a non-profit agency for cultural development in the Palm Beaches that provides grants and support to local artists and cultural organizations. As a member of the council, you'll receive invitations to member-only events and subscriptions to cultural council publications. You'll also meet plenty of people who share your interest in the arts.

Source: Capehart Photography
Palm Beachers mix and mingle at Evening on Antique Row,
benefitting the Young Friends of the Historical Society of Palm Beach County.

Of course, our county's many sports clubs, country clubs, and boat clubs are all great ways to meet people in a social setting as well.

Faith-based Organizations

Palm Beach County has numerous faith-based organizations to choose from. According to Share Faith, the leading Christian denominations in the county include Evangelical denominations, the Catholic Church, the United Methodist Church, and the Episcopal Church. The Archdiocese of Palm Beach provides numerous parishes throughout the county. For more information on local parishes, visit www.diocesepb. org. All Christians can view a list of nearby churches in their area by visiting www.sharefaith.com or www.churchfinder.com.

Perhaps the most famous church in the county is Palm Beach's historic **Bethesda-by-the-Sea Church.** The Episcopal church is the oldest place of worship and first Protestant church in the county. Bethesda-by-the-Sea features ornate stained glass windows, paintings, and sculptures throughout the structure. It also offers plenty of service opportunities, youth and adult programs, as well as Sunday School classes.

According to Movoto, Palm Beach County has roughly 255,000 Jewish residents. The majority of the area's Jewish population lives in the South County towns of Delray Beach, Boca Raton, and Boynton

Beach—according to *Hadassah Magazine*. Boca Raton is known for its **Temple Beth El**, which is the southeastern United State's largest Reform synagogue. To find more information about local synagogues and to get involved with the Jewish community in Palm Beach County, I suggest exploring **The Jewish Federation of South Palm Beach County** (www.tbeboca.org), the Mandel Jewish Community Center of the Palm Beaches (www.jcconline.com), and the Jewish Federation of Palm Beach County (www.jewishpalmbeach.org).

Voting

Voting requirements are what you might expect; one must be at least 18 years of age, a U.S. citizen, and a legal resident of Florida and the county. Voter registration applications are available online at the Palm Beach County Supervisor of Elections website at www.pbcelections.org/default.aspx. You can deliver the application by mail or in person to one of the local Supervisor of Elections' offices. You must also provide a valid Florida driver's license number or Florida identification card number. If you are without either of these, then you can provide the last four digits of your Social Security number.

An important note from your voting application:

"Florida is a closed primary election state. In primary elections, registered voters can only vote for their registered party's candidates in a partisan race on the ballot. In a primary election, all registered voters, regardless of party affiliation, can vote on any issue, nonpartisan race, and race where a candidate faces no opposition in the General Election. If you do not indicate your party affiliation, you will be registered with no party affiliation. For a list of political parties, visit the Division of Elections' website at: www.election.dos.state.fl.us/."

Establishing Residency

New Floridians automatically establish residency by registering to vote, placing a child in a Florida school or when they begin working in Florida. You can obtain and file a Declaration of Domicile with the office of the Clerk and Comptroller. To find more information about establishing residency, visit www.mypalmbeachclerk.com.

Registering Your Vehicle

All new residents must register their cars within 10 days of establishing residency. New residents are also required to get a Florida driver's license within 30 days. Before registering the vehicle, however, you will need Florida Auto Insurance. To find the nearest DMV to you, check the **Florida Department of Highway Safety and Motor Vehicles** website at www.hsmv.state.fl.us/offices/palmbeach.html.

Insider tip: You can go online to make an appointment for your driver's license at the local DMV, whereas other services (title, registration, etc.) require you to wait in line. Having all of your other paperwork in order while obtaining the license may allow you to complete those additional tasks, saving yourself a long wait on a return trip.

Local Media

Staying current on local news, happenings, and trends is an important part of moving to a new area. Here are a few of the many popular media sources in the Palm Beaches.

Print and Digital Newspapers

The Palm Beach Post – www.palmbeachpost.com

Palm Beach Daily News – www.palmbeachdailynews.com

Sun-Sentinel – www.sun-sentinel.com

The South Florida Business Journal – www.bizjournals.com/southflorida

Miami Herald – www.miamiherald.com

Florida Weekly – www.floridaweekly.com

Palms West Monthly – www.palmswestmonthly.com

El Latino Semanal – www.ellatinodigital.com

The Pineapple Newspaper – www.pineapplenewspaper.com

The Coastal Star – www.thecoastalstar.com

Town-Crier – www.gotowncrier.com

TC Palm – www.tcpalm.com

The Boca Raton Tribune – www.bocaratontribune.com

Print and Digital Magazines

Palm Beach Illustrated – www.palmbeachillustrated.com

Boca Raton Magazine – www.bocamag.com

Delray Beach Magazine – www.bocamag.com/blog/category/del-ray/

West Palm Beach Magazine – www.wpbmagazine.com

New Times Broward-Palm Beach – www.browardpalmbeach.com

Art & Culture Magazine – www.palmbeachculture.com

The Palm Beacher Magazine – www.palmbeachermagazine.com

PBG Lifestyle Magazine – www.pbglifestyle.com

City & Shore Magazine – www.cityandshore.com

Palm Beach Woman – www.palmbeachwoman.com

Palm Beach Society – www.pbsociety.com

Jupiter Magazine – www.jupitermag.com

Boca Life Magazine – www.bocalifemagazine.com

The Boca Raton Observer – www.bocaratonobserver.com

Atlantic Ave Magazine – www.atlanticavemagazine.com

Local Influencers to Follow on Twitter

City News

@InsideFPL – Florida Power & Light

@DowntownBoca – Downtown Boca Raton

@DowntownWPB – Downtown West Palm Beach

@westpalmbch – City of West Palm Beach

@CityofPBG – City of Palm Beach Gardens

@CityBocaRaton – City of Boca Raton

@TownofJupiter – Jupiter Town Government and Police Department

@LakeWorthPBC – City of Lake Worth

@Wellingtonflgov – Village of Wellington

@citydelraybeach – City of Delray Beach

@BoyntonBeachCRA – Boynton Beach CRA

@PBCountySheriff – Official account of Palm Beach County Sheriff's Office.

@SchoolPolicePBC – Palm Beach County School District Police Department

@myPBC – Palm Beach County

@cityplacewpb – City Place

@jmuoio – West Palm Beach Mayor Jeri Muoio

@pbcgov – Palm Beach County

@PBI_Airport – Palm Beach International Airport

@PalmBeachesFL – Palm Beach Convention and Visitors Bureau

@palmbchculture – Cultural Council of Palm Beach

@chamberupdate – The Chamber of Commerce of the Palm Beaches

@PalmBeachCivic – Palm Beach news and events

Lifestyle

@aGuyOnClematis – Aaron Wormus, West Palm Beach Blogger named 2011 "best blog in South Florida" by *Sun Sentinel.*

@ShopMiznerPark – Mizner Park

@MiznerParkAmphi – Mizner Amphitheater

@thingstodopb – Palm Beach Post Entertainment

@bocamag – Boca Raton Magazine

@visitwpb – West Palm Beach Magazine

@NewTimesBPBFood – Food news from the New Times Broward-Palm Beach

@LizBalmaseda – Food and Dining Editor of the Palm Beach Post

@LibbyShootsFood – Libby Volgyes, Local Food and Lifestyle Photographer

@PalmBeachLately – Palm Beach Lately Blog

@FlavorPalmBeach – Palm Beach Restaurant Week

CHAPTER THIRTEEN
ADDITIONAL NEWCOMER INFORMATION & RESOURCES

Moving Companies

Better Business Bureau Accredited Movers

www.bbb.org/south-east-florida/accredited-business-directory/movers

Better Business Bureau Accredited Car Transportation Services

www.bbb.org/south-east-florida/accredited-business-directory/auto-transporters-and-drive-away-companies

Newcomer Resources

Cable and TV Services

Comcast
1-800-COMCAST (1-800-266-2278)

AT&T (U-Verse)
1-800-288-2020
Hotwire

1-800-355-5668

Electric

Florida Power & Light
561-697-8000
www.fpl.com

Lake Worth Utilities
561-533-7300
www.lakeworth.org

Natural Gas

Florida Public Utilities
561-832-0872 or 800-427-7712
www.fpuc.com

Landline Telephone

AT&T
888-757-6500
www.att.com

Water

Palm Beach County Water Utilities
561-740-4600 and 561-278-5135
www.pbcwater.com

Garbage and Recyclable Collection

Solid Waste Authority of Palm Beach County
561-697-2700
www.swa.org

Emergency

Police and Fire Emergencies
Call 911

Poison Control Center
800-222-1222

County Division of Emergency Management
561-712-6400

Non-Emergency

Palm Beach County Sheriff's Office
561-688-3000

Boca Raton Police
561-338-1333

Boynton Beach Police
561-732-8116

Delray Beach Police
561-243-7800

Jupiter Police
561-746-6201

Lake Worth Police
561-586-1611

North Palm Beach Police
561-848-2525

Palm Beach Police
561-838-5454

Palm Beach Gardens Police
561-799-4445

Riviera Beach Police
561-845-4126

Wellington Police
561-688-5447

West Palm Beach Police
561-822-1600

Crime Prevention

Crime Stoppers
800-458-TIPS

Government Services

Tax Collector
561-355-2264
www.pbctax.com

Animal Control
561-233-1200
www.pbcgov.com/publicsafety/animalcare

City of West Palm Beach
561-659-8096
www.wpb.org

County Health Department
561-840-4500
www.palmbeach.floridahealth.gov

Florida Fish & Wildlife Conservation Commission
561-625-5122
www.myfwc.com

Florida Highway Patrol
561-357-4000
www.flhsmv.gov

Marriage Licenses
561-355-2986
www.mypalmbeachclerk.com

Palm Beach County Parks & Recreation
561-966-6600
www.pbcgov.com

Property Appraiser
561-355-3230
www.co.palm-beach.fl.us/papa

Supervision of Elections (Voter Registration)
561-656-6200
www.pbcelections.org

Veteran's Services
561-355-4761
www.pbcgov.com

Discover the Palm Beaches (Convention and Visitors Bureau)
561-233-3000
www.palmbeachfl.com

Business Development Board of Palm Beach County
561-835-1008
www.bdb.org

Palm Beach County Cultural Council
561-471-2901
www.palmbeachculture.com

Palm Beach County Sports Commission
561-233-3180
www.palmbeachsports.com

ACKNOWLEDGEMENTS

This book would never have come to fruition without the help of so many amazing Palm Beach residents, newfound friends, and of course, multiple pairs of eyes and ears. First, I want to thank the incredibly talented Libby McMillan, who introduced me to my publisher Newt Barrett of Voyager Media. A huge thanks to Newt for taking a chance on me. I'm forever grateful for the opportunity to explore my new home in such a unique way.

Thank you to our realtor, Darren Goldstein and his wife Elizabeth, for showing us the ins and outs of Central and North County. You opened our eyes to the fantastic way of life in Jupiter, Juno Beach, Palm Beach Gardens, Singer Island, and West Palm Beach. Thank you also to local realtor Bob Paul for spending an entire Saturday morning carting me around various South County neighborhoods. Your real estate insights and expert knowledge of the market were invaluable. Also, a big thanks to the infinitely helpful Ron Bill of Virtual Global Realty, for patiently answering all of my real estate questions (probably hundreds of them) with a smile on your face.

A deep bow of gratitude to my friend Susan Friedman, who convinced us that Delray Beach was the "place to be." You were right, of course. It ended up being the perfect spot for Justin and me. Thank you also for your encouragement and suggestions during my book writing process.

Thank you to Kelly Smallridge, president of the Business Development Board of Palm Beach County, for answering my questions and lending me your voice. Thanks to all of the businesses, PR pros, and towns in Palm Beach County that gave me their gorgeous snapshots. Thank you to my friend and uber-talented photographer Dana McMahon, who went above and beyond in helping me with photos. A huge thank you to all of my fabulous contributors as well—including: Caitlin Parker, Vicki Pugh, Sally Shorr, Steve Gallagher, and Audrey Bird. I'm truly honored and delighted to have been able to include you in this book. Thank you, also, to the Palm Beach savvy Enid Atwater for your help and generosity during this writing journey.

Thank you to all of my cheerleaders—without whom, this book would not have happened. Thank you to my friends and family – especially to my parents for always encouraging me to travel, explore, and step outside my comfort zone.

Finally, thank you to the sweetest cheerleader of all—my husband, Justin, who inspires me every day with his infectious positivity and zest for life. Just a short time ago, we were cooped up in our Boston apartment surrounded by 108 inches of snow. How far we've come!

ABOUT THE AUTHOR

Source: Dana McMahon

If anyone knows how to move successfully, it's Marian White.

The South Carolina native spent her 20's living and working in China, Washington, DC, New York City, and Boston before settling in Palm Beach County. With every move, she mastered the art of folding banker's boxes, repurposing bubble wrap, and unabashedly asking for directions. She also managed to dip her toes in an array of communication fields along the way including politics, hospitality, public relations, and journalism.

Most recently she was a lifestyle staff writer for a popular online news site in Boston, covering the city's food and dining scene. Marian wrote over 1,700 articles with a focus on restaurants, nightlife, innovative food-tech startups, and local events. Her work has been quoted in various media outlets including Eater, the Boston Business Journal, and Jezebel. In just two years, the author developed a loyal readership and managed to build a successful brand for herself in the Bay State. While living in Boston, she also earned her Master's Degree in global marketing communications from Emerson College.

Marian now lives an endless summer in Delray Beach, Florida with her husband Justin and pet poodle Henry. When not writing, you can find her exploring all of the best eats and outdoor activities that Palm Beach County has to offer.

Follow her on Twitter: @MarianEWhite
Reach her at MovingToPalmBeachCounty@gmail.com

More information on this book

Instagram: @movingtopalmbeachcounty
Book Website: www.MovingToPalmBeachCountyGuide.com
Facebook: www.facebook.com/movingtopalmbeach county
Twitter: @MovingtoPBC

NOTES

NOTES

Made in the USA
Middletown, DE
25 April 2017